The Poetic Ramblings of an Old Australian

KEN GOWER

This book is dedicated to my father
whose poem is last in the book

I'd like to thank my wife Lorraine and
daughter Pauline, without whose help, guidance
and assistance this book would not exist

First published in 2020 by Ken Gower

© Ken Gower 2020

The moral rights of the authors have been asserted

All enquiries should be made to the author

Printed in Australia by McPherson's Printing

Project management and design by Publish Central

Contents

Accident Prone

I went for a walk the other day
When I kicked an old tin can
But someone put a brick inside
Am I limping yes I am

I went to go into a shop
And walked through a plate glass door
Am I OK I am not
I'm limping and I'm sore

I walked beneath a ladder
While I was feeling faint
The painter dropped a great big can
And covered me with paint

I thought I'll get cleaned up
It can't be all that far
But crossing over the busy road
I'm run over by a car

They put me in the ambulance
I thought a change in luck
But halfway to the hospital
We collided with a truck

I woke up in emergency
And felt for broken bones
But I'm head to toe in plaster
And could only make some groans

Suddenly the orderlies shouting
The situation's dire
Try and get the patients out
The hospital's on fire

So I'm laying in the car-park
Feeling pretty ill
When the brake slipped on my trolley
And I took off down the hill

Down I went at breakneck speed
Am I praying? Yes I am
Then I crashed into a great big wall
And I landed with a slam

My plaster cracked
My trolley broke up
From unconsciousness
I slowly woke up

Then I saw it lying there
That rusty old tin can
I couldn't resist temptation
Am I limping? Yes I am

The Silent Traveller

He travelled down the freeway
Turned off at a country lane
The dawn was bright and sunny
Without the hint of rain

He passed by the farmers
Working on their crop
But the vehicle he was riding in
Just did not want to stop

He travelled down the byways
Over hill and dale
But his vehicle kept on going
Like a train upon the rail

He passed by some villagers
Some who stopped and stared
But the driver of the vehicle
Just turned his head and glared

They stopped outside a little church
Inside nice words were read
The people stood around his coffin
As he lay inside, quite dead

They took him to the cemetery
Inside his family tomb
I suppose you could almost liken it
To being back in his mother's womb

He lay there in the darkness
Surrounded by his kin
And his body slowly withered
To just some bones and skin

But the villagers still whisper
Of the man they buried there
Of the wooden stake right through his heart
Does the thought give you a scare?

The Truckies

You know when you see those huge great trucks
Roaring down the road
Pulling two huge trailers
Carrying a massive load

The truckie has a responsibility
To make sure all is well
Not to cause an accident
And send us all to hell

Some of them like to tailgate
Their trucks so close and near
You look back in your mirrors
And all you feel is fear

They seem to think the road is theirs
And we're just in the way
We know they have to earn a living
But is the danger worth the pay

But some of those trucks are beautiful
With paint all bright and shiny
When they stop at the lights beside you
They make you feel so tiny

But there are others that are ugly
All dirt and belching smoke
Driven by some dickhead
A really nasty bloke

We know most of them are good guys
Who drive quite safe upon our roads
They drive within the limits
And know they carry heavy loads

The big trucks are important
Most drivers are first class
But tell the bloody dickheads
To stay back off my arse

A Gentleman Asleep

I sit here writing this poem
About my Grandson Matt
He passed away some weeks ago
But I don't want to dwell on that

The future is what we look for
And Matt would want that too
Myself, his Mum Pauline
And all the rest of you

Matt was just a lovely bloke
He always gave his all
Anyone with a problem
Would just give Matt a call

Now Matt just loved his motorbike
I think a Suzuki Marauder
He loved his job as manager
As he left everything in order

Charity work Matt loved most
And we know that love was real
For the hours and hours he put in
Spending time on his company's appeal

His favourite colour was purple
Strange colour for a man
Just wear some on the 8th April
Please do the best you can

His Mum Pauline was proud of him
He was her tower of strength
And when his Mum was need of him
He would go to any length

In closing off these words of mine
I would really like to say
'Cheers fella' and 'No wukkas mate'
I'm sure we'll meet again one day

Twisters

Out in America's mid west
Is a place they call storm alley
Where the twisters all come flying through
And the damage you can't tally

There's piles and piles of debris
And a lot of lives are lost
With houses and vehicles piled
Where by the wind they're tossed

Some have lost their roofing
Some have lost their homes
You can tell the ones that lost the most
By their faces and their groans

People seem to stand around
Their faces all gone blank
Everything they own gone missing
Except that useless water tank

They come without much warning
And given little time
They come roaring on the township
With a frightening sort of whine

The people look for shelter
You can almost feel their fright
As the storm rages down upon them
With all its immeasurable might

But the people of the mid west
Are made of sterner stuff
Their courage comes to the fore
When the going gets really tough

The twisters rage right through storm alley
And down upon the townships burst
The people there display their courage
And know that they've survived the worst

The Swagman

He wakes up in the morning
And heads towards the road
He sleeps where he can lay his head
He has no real abode

His skin is dry
His hands are rough
The life he leads
Is really tough

He needs to find his breakfast
To set him for the day
The weather's going to be really hot
He may walk a very long way

He quickly snares a rabbit
And brews his billy-tea
There's not a living soul about
As far as he can see

Soon he puts his gear away
In a little gunny sack
Everything the Swagman owns
Is carried on his back

Always alert as he walks along
He's hoping for some luck
The next town is a long way off
Perhaps a lift from a passing truck

He's been on the road for many years
And his days are nearly done
He needs an act of kindness
Will he ever meet that kind someone

The days are getting longer
And he doesn't move as fast
He knows the time is getting close
When he may breathe his last

So he wanders off the highway
Lays down his weary head
He stayed just there for many years
That's where we found him, dead

The Motor Car

Do you drive a motor car
And does it guzzle fuel
Have you ever thought of changing
Till all its fuel is dual

The world we know is changing
And climate change is here
Why not change to a cleaner fuel
It's nowhere near as dear

We have to be so careful
Of everything we do
Not send pollutants in the air
That can't be good for you

Do we want our children
To blame us for their lot
Or do we now look after
The wonderful world we've got

You don't have to use your motor car
When its only a short walk to go
You might even end up healthier
Try it then you'll know

Its silly seeing one person
In a great big motor car
Try and get a lift with them
We'll be better off by far

The experts say they want you
To try and take a hike
Perhaps you aren't quite able to
And you can't afford a bike

But what ever it is you do
The future we can't mar
We must cut down the usage
Of that pollution spreading motor car

The Sounds of Silence

I'm looking out the window
At all the green around
I'm standing here in silence
Nothing makes a sound

I can't hear any noises
No birds can I hear sing
I can see one in the distance
Out there on the wing

I can't hear any lawnmowers
Engines belching smoke
Can't even hear a Jumbo Jet
It's silence, like a cloak

Can't hear any kids
Playing in the street
Can't hear the sounds of football
When they kick it with their feet

No neighbours arguing over the fence
Tranquillity reigns supreme
Can't hear the roaring of the crowd
When they yell and shout and scream

The factories seem silent
Although the men are there
They seem to be all working
But I just stand and stare

Can't hear the farmers' tractors
When they're out there with the ploughs
Can't hear the farm machinery
When they work to milk the cows

I can't hear my wife calling
When she's in another room
Can't hear the bees all buzzing
As around the yard they zoom

I can't hear any music
From radio or TV
No leaves rustling in the trees
As far as I can see

I can't hear any noises
From anything that's made
I think I need a battery
For my worn out hearing aid

The Pennant Final

You pick your bowl up off the ground
And you stand upon the mat
Your Skip calls out, down this side
But you don't think much of that

You take your aim and release the bowl
It goes sailing on it's way
Flies past Kitty and in the ditch
What does a bowler say

Your opponent bowls his up real close
The Skipper says to drive
You let it go with all your might
He's lucky to be alive

It hits the Skipper on the foot
And he falls upon his back
He scatters all the other bowls
They don't think much of that

Up comes the umpire
There's chaos on the mat
Your Skipper's down amongst the bowls
Flat upon his back

The umpire says in all my life
I've never seen this done
I'm sure that you are five shots up
That means your team has won

You all start to celebrate
The other team just moans
You all shake each other's hand
The Skip lies there and groans

You're interviewed by the newspaper
About the shot that won the match
But wait a sec there's something wrong
There seems to be a catch

Someone shakes you by the shoulder
And taps you on the head
Will you stop bloody dreaming
And get up out of bed

A Father's Story

Do you remember years ago
When you were just a child
Wouldn't do as you were told
And made your parents wild

Remember when you went outside
Played cricket in the street
Swung the bat as hard as you could
Making ball and window meet

As you grew up it got quite serious
About the sport you want to play
You hope to be a footballer
And star in the AFL one day

Then you met your partner
Which completely changed your life
One day you would have children
And they would be no strife

You worked hard for your family
And did for them your best
You were a good provider
And the good lord did the rest

You were blessed with lovely children
Two daughters and a son
Your daughters were just beautiful
And your son was loved by everyone

The girls they both got married
To well known business men
They both blessed you with grandkids
Life could not be better then

Your son became a giant
In business and in stature
He helped all those in need of him
Everyone seemed to matter

Then came the day he said to you
Dad I hope you take this well
I've been selected for the firsts
I'm playing in the AFL

The Unseen Danger

Well it seems we have a visitor
Very small and can't be seen
We need to take precautions
This thing is quite obscene

We have to wear a mask
Don't breathe other people's breath
To do so could be dangerous
It could even mean your death

Some idiots refuse to wear them
But it's only just a few
They're being very foolish
They could end up in ICU

A few that tested positive
And broke the lockdown rule
Should take a look in the mirror
They'd be looking at a fool

I could go on for hours
It's a subject without end
The rules are made for our safety
And not for fools to bend

I wish everyone health and happiness
And all of you take care
Remember all the dangers
Of that visitor in the air

Keep well everyone and look after your families

A Bowling Partnership

We started off just playing bowls
It's social and it's sport
We have a lot of fun here
Even when our bowling comes to naught

Our first year was a good one
We sometimes had a win
Forgot about the weather though
Got sunburnt on our skin

We learnt to get the bowl
Up fairly close to kitty
And when you're soundly beaten
Not to get too shitty

We both then got selected
To play in the Pennant teams
Other members took us aside
And told us what this means

Both of you will each play lead
And start to build the head
Listen to what your skipper says
And do everything he said

Now when you play a long end
And your skipper starts to mutter
Bloody, stupid, silly sod
You've put it in the gutter

Just smile and take your aim once more
Then bowl it from the mat
You've bowled a resting toucher
And the skip lifts up his hat

We feel we're really members
Of this club by the babbling brook
We help the club as much as we can
With the jobs we've undertook

We hope the club will grow
And get bigger every year
So if you want some social sport
Come and join us all down here

Standing in the Kitchen

I was standing in the kitchen
Just looking around the place
My mind turned to thinking about
All the problems that we face

We've got trouble all around the world
With wars that never end
Afghanistan and Iraq
More troops we seem to send

Our world is getting hotter
Our farms are very dry
We're chopping down the living trees
Sending pollution way up high

Gangs are getting stronger
Oblivious to the law
We don't have enough resources
Where do we go for more

We've over fished the oceans
To satisfy our greed
We need to build more fish farms
Another thing we need

Methane gas from cattle
Pollution from our cars
If we keep going in this vane
We may have to move to Mars

If the money and the energy
That we spend and use on sport
Was spent on fixing problems
Those wars would not be fought

I'm just standing in the kitchen
Looking around the place
What will I have for dinner
That's the problem that I face

Merlin the Magician

In a time long since past
Dragons flew over our skies
Witches cast their magic spells
And to fame one man would rise

He was a Master Magician
Merlin was his name
He made his base at Camelot
That's where he made his fame

Arthur was the English King
And Guinevere his Queen
Behind them both was Merlin
His presence felt but seldom seen

He could turn a stick into a snake
Or a man into a toad
He lived for many hundred years
Though he carried such a heavy load

He thought the safety of the kingdom
Rested solely on his shoulders
He got the King to build an army
Of thousands and thousands of soldiers

Behind the scenes Sir Lancelot
Had an affair with Guinevere
The King had placed his trust in him
He was the King's first peer

The King took away his knighthood
And from the realm was banished
From that day forth forever
Sir Lancelot just vanished

Then came the war of sixty-six
On the day that Arthur died
Someone shot an arrow in the air
And it struck him in the eye

William became the Norman King
And Merlin moved away
Where he went no-one knows
At least no-one will say

Now no-one knows where Camelot was
It's impossible to find
And if you think that you might know
Then Merlin's in your mind

The Pokies

Do you like to play the pokies
Just sit there on your own
Put your money in the slot
I can almost hear you groan

You hope to win some money
But it's usually in vain
But somehow they draw you back
Again and again and again

You sometimes get the feature
But it doesn't pay a lot
It supplements what you've got left
Do you go home? You do not

It's as if you're in a different world
You feel like time's stood still
You're hypnotised by flashing lights
Will you keep playing? Yes you will

Very slowly your luck begins to change
You're in a winning zone
You don't have to share your money
You're glad you're on your own

You feel at last your day has come
To get some losses back
But they slowly eat away your cash
It seems you've lost the knack

All the machines are busy
You stay just where you are
And the people that are next to you
Are all in front by far

You put up the reserved sign
And to the toilet go
Then get a cup of coffee
Your excitement starts to show

You sit down once more, begin to play
But your money's going fast
You open up your wallet
And hope that it's the last

You know it's happened many times
You really should go home
But you may as well play some more
Because now you're living on your own

A Game of Golf Perhaps

You're taken to play a game of golf
A most frustrating game
If you decide to take it up
Your life won't ever be the same

You step on to the first tee
Put your ball on a wooden spike
Drive it down the fairway
Then you take a hike

Eventually you reach the green
You've played with heart and soul
Then they bloody tell you
You've got to putt it in the hole

You think the par three hole is easier
Than the par four that you've done
But you put it in the bunker
I say good luck to you my son

Then off you go on a long par five
And you drive it in the rough
You feel that you should pack it in
But you're made of sterner stuff

You hack it out after a few more goes
Straight in to the lake
Your partners say oh that's bad luck
But a penalty you'll take

Your temper's getting shorter now
You're doing the best you can
This game is so frustrating
Nothing goes to plan

Then you get the driver out
And go down on your knees
Please lord help me drive it straight
But you put it in the trees

That's it you shout you've had enough
There's eighteen bloody holes
You throw your clubs in to the lake
And take up playing bowls

Heroes of the CFA

It arrived quite suddenly
With gale force winds and heat
We know that we're in trouble
When bush and firebugs meet

It roared down on the townships
They never stood a chance
With water from a garden hose
They couldn't stop the fire's advance

Some chose to stand and fight the fire
Others chose to run
Now people search the ruins
Looking for a lost someone

Some died with loved ones in their arms
Others in their cars were caught
Some died trying to save their pets
It was safety that they sought

The Firemen of the CFA
Are the heroes we must thank
Fighting to halt the inferno
As all our spirits sank

Callignee, Narbethong and Wandong
Are towns no longer there
Strathewen, Marysville and Kinglake
Were where the Earth's now bare

Helicopters dropping water bombs
Fireballs making awful sounds
Infernos race towards them
But the CFA still stand their ground

Is there a lesson to be learnt?
From when the winds and fires arrive
Will we still lose more townships?
Will some townsfolk not survive?

We hope you've learnt some lessons
Listened to what the experts say
And give a great big thank you
To the fighting men of the CFA

Let's try and help the people
Who've lost everything they own
Let's help them know we're here with them
That they are not alone

Let them clear an area around their house
And keep the trees away
Let them live in safety
I think the Greens have had their say

Riding on a Broom

I know a person short in stature
Who likes to ride a broom
She started off just slowly
Flying around the room

But now she's really good at it
And fly's around the town
The people stare as she flies by
And wave as she goes round

Although she's good at flying
She finds it hard to land
She usually ends up on her bum
Though she's supposed to stand

Her husband is a patient man
He puts up with so much
Her broom hangs like a trophy
That he's not allowed to touch

She went down to the sportsman's club
And thought she'd go by broom
But she flew across the firing range
And heard the guns go boom

Suddenly she's in a spin
Someone scored a hit
She can't control that ruddy broom
I don't like this one bit

She crashed into a paddock
Then dusted herself down
She's covered in this brown stuff
There's cow patts all around

That's it, her husband said
Your broom has broke in half
They'll be no more flying for you my girl
She said don't be so bloody daft

She crept out to the garden
He says this looks pretty suss
There she was up and down
Riding on the toilet brush

Global Warming

Global warming is a problem
That worsens every day
Let's call in some experts
The pollies have had their say

Is it a question of money
Does big business make the rules
Will the children of the future
Think that we were fools

Millions of tons of pollution
Are in the atmosphere
It's alright making money
But is the cost too dear?

The ice caps slowly melting
Means the sea will surely rise
Will someone tell the truth to us
Or continue with their lies

We should stop using fossil fuels
Use the energy of the sun
But they can't sell that energy
'Cos it's free to everyone

We could use the power of the wind
Tidal movements of the sea
We must help future generations
It's up to you and me

Droughts are getting worse
Our land is getting dry
But we don't have the time to stop
Reflect and wonder why

We must stop felling our forests
Then replace the trees
It's up to the people of all nations
We can't do as we please

Our Feathered Friends

Have you ever listened?
When you are sitting quiet
To the singing of our birds
You really ought to try it

Have you ever listened?
When the Robin starts his song
Or the caw caw of the crow
As he seems to strut along

Have you ever seen a hawk
As he dives upon his prey
Trying to catch his dinner
So he can live another day

Have you heard an owl
As he hoots away at night
Or been swooped on by a magpie
Now that gives you a fright

Have you seen a swan
Majestic as he swims
Or our pink and grey galahs
As they argue in the limbs

Have you ever seen an eagle
As across our skies they soar
Have you ever fed the seagulls
Always wanting more

Have you ever seen an emu
Or our famous cockatoo
Have you seen a pelican
Or that Wren that's coloured blue

But I must admit my favourite
Is our family of rosellas
All the colours of the rainbow
Beautiful little fellas

The Zoological Band

When I took the family to the zoo
Some strange things happened there
The first one we ran into
Was a great big grizzly bear

None of the animals were locked up
Just free to browse and roam
All the staff had done a bunk
And we were on our own

An elephant came strolling past
A conductor's wand in hand
Blowing a tuba with his trunk
Followed by the zoo's big band

A silver backed gorilla was next
Playing a slide trombone
Followed by lots of animals
With instruments of their own

A baboon was right behind him
He looked really cute
Marching to the rhythm
That he made on his flute

Then along came rhinos
Banging on their drums
Then guitar playing chimpanzees
Plucking with their thumbs

The hippos too were in the band
The violins they played
Some lions were playing trumpet
What a noise they made

A giraffe was marching in the group
Playing a double base
With a leopard there playing a harp
I'm sure this was the case

A tiger played his organ
A zebra played the clarinet
The warthogs played the bagpipes
They were the best ones yet

All the animals followed
The deer, koala and kangaroo
But we need more animals playing instruments
Could we count on YOU

Credit Card Debt

Have you got a credit card
And are you deep in debt
Do you try and pay a bit each week
After other bills are met

Does the bank send you your statement
Saying what you owe
Can you meet the rising interest rate
From the rotten so and so

So you're struggling with your credit card
And with mortgage payments too
Is all this debt a bit too much
For you to struggle through

Do you pray for a win on lotto
To try and help you out
If you go without your dinner
Then I'm afraid there is no doubt

You're way too over committed
With a debt you can't afford
You've got to cut your spending
Right across the board

No more take-away food at night
No restaurants any time
Don't be tempted by a bargain
No hire-purchase will you sign

Common sense is what it takes
Total commitment all the time
You must reduce that statement total
Just a little line by line

Have you done your sums and worked it out
Just what you can pay
You know it will only happen slowly
If you take it day by day

These words are meant to encourage you
To reduce your rising debt
If you take on board a few of them
There's some hope for you yet

The Barfly

He walks in to the bar
And orders a couple of drinks
He knows he can handle plenty
At least that's what he thinks

They sit around a table
Consuming more and more
Just like in the old days
But no sawdust on the floor

His mates slowly drift on home
To see their patient wives
But he's got no-one at his place
His mates lead different lives

The night wears on
He's not that steady
He won't go home
Until he's ready

We've all heard that saying
Just one more for the road
But he doesn't live by those rules
He lives by the barfly's code

The landlord says last orders
But his drinking's not yet done
And as he's leaving to go home
He buys a bottle of rum

He staggers out to the cold night air
He knows it's not too far
From his pocket he gets his keys
The fool has got a car

But someone's waiting in the car-park
And from him takes his keys
Tonight he says I'll drive you home
You're just not safe with these

He lays slowly on his bed
His mind is just a fog
He opens up his bottle of rum
He needs a hair of the dog

He wakes around mid morning
Goes down to his car
Parks it in the car-park
Then he walks in to the bar

Our Home Australia

Australia is our country
An island huge and vast
With a long and varied history
And mystery in our past

There's mountain streams and rapids
Where thousands panned for gold
There's paintings in the wilderness
We just don't know how old

There's miles and miles of beaches
For lying in the sun
But remember melanoma
The sun forgives no-one

There's snow capped mountain ranges
Where people love to ski
There's dark forbidding rainforests
Most people never see

There's Bungle Bungles and Uluru
Owned by the local tribes
There's a place called Hanging Rock
That gives out such strange vibes

Of course we have Tasmania
An island sweet and green
Some of the scenery seen there
Is the best you've ever seen

The wildlife in our country
Is unique around the world
Animals with pouches
And lizard's frills unfurled

The solitary platypus
The world's most deadly snake
The saltwater crocodile
All make our country great

The migrants, aborigines and settlers
All live hand in hand
We all negotiate our problems
That's what makes our country grand

The Butterfly

The butterfly is a beautiful thing
As it flies from bush to tree
She lays her eggs beneath the leaves
Where you and I can't see

They lay there for a little while
And then caterpillars form
They munch away as fast as they can
Eating up a storm

Suddenly they stop
Then spin a little web
They hang inside a small cocoon
And look as if they're dead

But wait a while a surprise will come
As they enter a brand new world
They leave their little brown cocoon
With their beautiful wings unfurled

The butterfly is a beautiful thing
As it flies from bush to tree
The most beautiful living creature
That anyone could see

Public Transport

Have you ever driven to the station?
Parked your car and gone by train
Done your shopping or been to work
And then caught it home again

Train travel can be convenient
If you use a little thought
You won't have to sit at traffic lights
And in queues of cars you won't be caught

You won't have to sit behind
A truck that's belching smoke
You'll get to work all clean and fresh
Like other city folk

Perhaps it's better for you
If you caught the local bus
You'll be sitting with other people
But there won't be any fuss

Whichever mode of transport
You choose to sit and travel
You can do sudoku or a crossword
Their mysteries to unravel

Just think, no more chance of road rage
No more looking where to park
No more parking meters
No more driving in the dark

There won't be any cameras
To catch you if you speed
There won't be any traffic wardens
There won't be any need

So just sit back in comfort
You won't be on your own
Let others do the driving
You can even use your phone

You'd be saving on your petrol
Less pollution in the air
Just climb on board and sit down
Make sure you pay your fare

If bus or train don't suit you
You've not done all you can
There's one more public transport
You can always catch the tram

Robin Hood

Robin Hood was a bandit
In the city of Nottingham
He robbed the rich, gave to the poor
A hero was that man

He lived in Sherwood Forest
With the Merry Men his band
There was Friar Tuck, and Little John
And Will Scarlett lent a hand

But Robin Hood loved Marion
A woman sweet and fair
He wanted to get in her in his bed
But he knew he wouldn't dare

A rich man travelled through the forest
He was the Sheriff's man
They robbed him of his jewels and clothes
As only Robin can

The Sheriff lost his temper
Yelled, assemble all the men
We're going to search all Sherwood
And find that Robbers' Den

They charged in to the forest
Not knowing what to do
They saw a man selling ice cream
And his sign said form a queue

They got down off their horses
And stood there all in line
When the Merry Men surrounded them
You should have heard the Sheriff whine

Robin told the Sheriff
You're a traitor to the King
All of you take your clothes off
And let us see your thing

The Men all started laughing
At a sight you couldn't beat
All the Sheriff's soldiers
With their trousers round their feet

Maid Marion had a good look
Her eyes stared straight ahead
She said I've changed my mind dear Robin
Let's get in your bed

Superman

Clark Kent was born on Krypton
As far as I can tell
His father sent him on a spaceship
His nappies made the planet smell

He landed near the town of Largeville
In America's mid west
Mrs Kent found him in a paddock
I'll try and tell you all the rest

She told her husband Jonathon
This baby's very strong
I know, he said I can smell him from here
Do you think that something's wrong

Then when he reached his manhood
They noticed something new
He wore a leotard beneath his clothes
And it was coloured blue

He got a job on a newspaper
And there he met Lois Lane
They only slept together once
He wouldn't do that again

If there was a world disaster
He stripped to his suit of blue
Then took a jump into the air
I think that's when he flew

He could fly all around the world
He could stop a runaway train
And if there was a problem in the air
He could even save a plane

He defeated the Joker, Juggler and Penguin
And all the crooks between
He was the greatest hero
The world had ever seen

Then he told his Mum and Jonathon
It was time he had to go
He had to build an icy palace
Up there in the snow

The population loved him
Built a statue to that man
The inscription underneath it read
A real life hero Batman

A Picnic at the Lake

We planned to go on a picnic
Out to a lovely lake
We made a list of all the things
That we would need to take

Off we went with our two kids
I'm glad it wasn't far
We only got to our corner
Didn't fix the trailer on our car

We soon fixed that little problem
And got there safe and sound
But we set down on an ants' nest
And the kids all jumped around

Right, she said, lets have some lunch
And out came all the food
Then a couple went strolling past us
And they were in the nude

My wife stood up and raised her leg
And gave my foot a stamp
She said, you stupid idiot
We're in a nudist camp

I gave a sort of bluster
And gave the bloke a wink
I said I'm sorry darling
I didn't even think

She said, you rotten devil
You knew this all along
We're stuck here in a nudist camp
What ever else is going wrong

I said, now listen darling
Seeing how we're stuck
Lets take all our clothes off
It's bound to change our luck

I suppose you're right, she said
We'll do it as you please
As she took her top off
Along came a swarm of bees

Her boobs bouncing, she took off
My son gave me a smile
My daughter was after her mother
I think they'll be gone for quite a while

So if you're going to a nudist lake
Don't get into strife
We may meet up there some time
I'll be looking for my wife

My Prize Winning Ute

I went to the pub the other day
I thought just a couple of beers
I walked in the bar, a great big crowd
And all of them yelling cheers

What's going on? I didn't know
They said you've won a new ute
Mine was a bomb, kept going wrong
I thought a new one sounds quite beaut

So we all of us had quite a party
To celebrate the ute that I'd won
My parents called in and gave me a hug
And said good luck to you son

My girlfriend said let's take a trip
To somewhere quite far away
It's a while 'til you get it
So let's plan a real special stay

We planned to go to Tamworth
Where they muster all the utes
Thousands and thousands of vehicles
Some of them massive great brutes

Then we'd go to Queensland
And lay there in the sun
And reflect upon how lucky we were
To ride in the ute that I'd won

We carefully made our plans
And studied all the maps
Tried to make sure we wouldn't
Fall into those travelling traps

The day was getting closer
When I'd go and collect my prize
I said to my girl I'm certain
This will open everyone's eyes

But when we went to the dealership
I kicked up a hell of a stink
It was a little four cylinder Suzuki
And the bloody thing was pink

Safe Borders

There's a lot of vermin in Australia
Brought from overseas
It seems the early immigrants
Could bring in what they pleased

Rabbits are a bad one
They do a lot of harm
Digging burrows everywhere
Ruining the farm

They breed so many times a year
So difficult to control
We've tried so many different baits
Even bulldozed all their holes

But there is a decent rabbit
They face a similar fate
We eat them all at Easter
They're made of chocolate

The fox is another visitor
A cruel and heartless beast
He'll kill all your chickens
But just take one for his feast

They love the lambing season
Will kill a new born lamb
They don't give him much trouble
And he'll eat all he can

The government offered a bounty
Ten dollars for each one
But I don't think they pay it now
They wanted money for their superannuation

Controls are so much better now
With inspections at our border
Stopping seeds and skins and plants
Keeping everything in order

We have to thank our customs men
For all the work they do
Trying to keep our country clean
For the likes of me and you

So thanks to those at the airport
And at the docks as well
For all the work you do for us
I think you're really swell

Skiing Down the Mountain

I'd like to take you skiing
Up into the snow
Winter's really with us now
So I know just where to go

We'll put on our warm clothing
And on each foot a ski
First we'll try the beginner's slope
Weeeheeeweee

We're going pretty fast now
Ahead I see a stump
You put a ski each side of it
And I hear a kind of thump

You roll around in agony
You don't have any choice
I thought you were singing opera
In a loud soprano voice

Next day you say you're ready
To do it all once more
I said will you be alright
You walk as if you're sore

Now we're on the expert's run
Somehow you lose a ski
You can't control direction
And crash into a tree

You're lying there in a tangled heap
Underneath a branch
Suddenly you're swept away
By a great big avalanche

We quickly chase down after you
And you seem to be ok
You said is there a problem
When my feet face the other way

You spend some time in hospital
Your feet are back in place
I suggest that maybe next time
We'll try a ski boat race

The Ski Boat Race

Well, we're in the Southern Eighty
That famous race on skis
There's lots of other racers
Who all do as they please

The race begins at 10 AM
We assemble there at nine
I know you're inexperienced
But I'm sure that you'll be fine

Now we'll have to check our gear
And I'm certain that you know
That skis we need for water
Are not the ones for snow

Our boat is very powerful
So make sure that you're right
When the starter fires his starting gun
You're hanging on real tight

The race is underway now
And we're really going fast
We're running in the middle
We're certainly not last

We go charging up the river
Skiers all in line
But watch out for other racers
Don't get your ropes entwined

We've got to just about the half way stage
And we're starting to look good
Is it possible to get a podium
I really think we could

We've passed some other skiers
Perhaps they've broken down
Their boats dead in the water
They've lost the winner's crown

With outboard motors screaming
We're in line, five abreast
The finish lines in sight now
Will the engines stand the test

We fly across the finish line
The judge's finger beckons
He says congratulations
Your boat has finished second

An Enchanted Forest

There is an Enchanted Forest
In a land that's far away
And although I don't know where it is
I hope to go there one fine day

They say there's lots of witches
And wizards live there as well
But all the witches are white ones
And always cast good spells

There's birds of every colour
And owls that hoot at night
But there's nothing there to scare you
You'll never get a fright

It's got a huge Enchanted Castle
With a handsome King and Queen
There's dogs that fly and cats that laugh
In this place we've never seen

Everyone there is happy
Their lives are not like mine
They don't know what unhappiness is
And there isn't any crime

The trees can walk and move around
And the flowers always bloom
The children play and are happy there
There is no need for gloom

There's animals we've never seen
And fish of every hue
If you listen very carefully
They'll even talk to you

They say the King and Queen
Are hundreds of years old
But no-one asks just how much
They'd never be so bold

There is an Enchanted Forest
That no-one's ever seen
And no-one ever will I fear
'Cos it's only just a dream

Our Birth

We started off as animals
Living in the trees
But we've got four fingers and a thumb
And only apes have these

Eventually we came down
To live upon the ground
But still we stayed on four legs
As we foraged all around

We learnt to walk on hind legs
And sat around the fires we made
We learnt to fashion stone tools
The foundation of mankind was made

Soon we started hunting
Game was all around
Animals were plenty
A community we'd found

There were earthquakes and volcanoes
Storms so loud and wild
Our world was not established
The earth was just a child

There were dinosaurs and pterodactyls
Some carnivorous and some not
They'd dominate the landscape
Until they got their lot

No one knows just why they went
But we knew when they disappeared
We'd start to grow in leaps and bounds
Mankind had just appeared

Next came language and the Iron Age
And villages in one spot
We were really growing now
Mankind could bless their lot

Now we're in the 21st century
Living in the modern era
While wars and troubles all abound
Why can't we live together

The Marathon Man

Would you like to run a marathon
The longest running race
To stand there at the starting line
Determined to take your place

But before you ever get there
Make sure you're really fit
You mustn't pull out halfway through
You will look like a twit

First you start off slowly
You mustn't do too much
Then increase it just a little
Enjoy the exercise as such

Each day you go out running
Further every time
You must make sure you're right on song
When you stand at the starting line

So now you think you're ready
And the race is almost due
You do your warm-up exercise
Ready to start on cue

The starter's gun has fired
The race is underway
You're running near the front
This could be just your day

The lead changes many times
You're up with the best
You're just behind the leaders
Way up on the rest

The race is halfway over
You're feeling pretty good
Make sure you keep the liquid up
Like all good runners would

The marathon's nearly run now
You're up there near the lead
You try to quicken up your pace
Can your legs withstand the speed

You're ready to chest the tape now
You suck the air in deep
Your wife yells out 'will you shut up
You're snoring in your sleep'

A Career in Politics

Would you like to be a politician
Sitting on your bum
Working down in Canberra
Making laws for everyone

You could have great big long discussions
About anything you choose
And whatever decision you come to
The public's gonna lose

You could increase taxation
That always goes down well
With your fellow politicians
Do you care if people yell

Don't worry about the pensioners
They're old and don't eat much
You don't care about the grey vote
But you're sadly out of touch

We remember the last election
You gave us money that was grand
But further on down the track
You took it with the other hand

Now what about an overseas trip
You work four days in seven
You could take a delegation
To some Caribbean heaven

You'll need to shake a hand or two
And have some conversation
Then it's into the bar, a dry martini
And heaps of relaxation

A week or two and home you come
You've got a year for your report
Then write a lot of dialogue
This is better than playing sport

Then very quick four years go by
You fight the next election
Suddenly you've got no job
You're suffering from rejection

There'll probably be a job for the boys
You've worked without aggravation
If there's just one word that makes you smile
It's superannuation

The Pensioners' Plight

How'd you like to be a Pensioner
No one listens to what you say
Living frugal to pay the bills
Roll on pension day

The Government no longer worries
Your usefulness has passed
You retired with little savings
But that's not going to last

Prescription costs are rising
And look at the price of fuel
You can't afford a luxury
Life can be so cruel

The Government gets huge rises
They really don't deserve
You're living on a pittance
You've spent all your reserves

They come up with a budget
Tax cuts was the call
Something for the Pensioners
We got none at all

You've worked hard all your life
Helped make this country great
Don't listen to their rhetoric
You got nothing mate

Perhaps we should form an army
Then take off all our clothes
Block the traffic in the streets
Will you be one of those

It will take some desperate measures
To make them see the light
We must convince these politicians
To understand our plight

A lot of them are millionaires
Not desperate for a dollar
We have to make them stop and listen
When all the Pensioners holler

Perhaps we'll meet at Parliament House
These Politicians should be booed
The whole grey army standing there
All booing partly nude

The Backseat Romance

I took my girlfriend parking
To try out my new van
And when we started kissing
She said I think we can

I ran my fingers down her back
She gave a sort of wiggle
Then when I kissed her on the neck
She gave a sort of giggle

We really started kissing
Our mouths were open wide
She gave me quite a shock when
She put her tongue inside

She undid a couple of buttons
Put her hand inside my shirt
Then told me in a husky voice
Help me with my skirt

Quickly we were naked
And then the fun began
There was someone loudly knocking
On the back doors of the van

I peeked out through the windows
And really got a shock
Her father with a shotgun
And both the hammers cocked

My ardour was diminished
I scrambled for my clothes
My girlfriend lying on the floor
Naked to her toes

Suddenly she shouted
Get off and start to drive
How the hell were we to know
Her father would arrive

Off we went driving fast
Determined to get away
But surrounded by police cars
What does a naked couple say

One of them grabbed hold of me
And gave me quite a shake
Will you get your pyjamas on
Mum shook me, wide-awake

Waterwise

Our water comes down from the sky
Disguised as pouring rain
But our storages are drying up
Will we ever see that rain again?

All our storage lakes
Are just a great big puddle
While our water minister waffles on
I think he's in a muddle

There must be some alternative
To what we are doing now
Our farmers stopped from planting crops
With only dust to plough

We could pump it from the Nullarbor
There's plenty under there
We could pump it down from Sydney
They get rain to spare

Most of the rain that falls
Just runs out to sea
There must be a way of saving it
For use by you and me

You can't take it from our place
If there's not much water there
And pump it down to Melbourne
'Cos we've got none to spare

They're going to run a pipeline
From Bendigo to Ballarat
And the Maryborough district?
We'll get none of that

They say it's really needed
Or Ballarat is lost
But why should we in Maryborough
Have to share the cost

The Drought

The drought stays with us now
As our farmland turns to dust
Some farmers walking off their land
Others just gone bust

Taking water from the rivers
The farmers allocated less
It's a problem for the country
And the government must confess

They take the lifeblood of the country
To water gardens down in town
You drive through the district
And shake your head and frown

Our lakes and dams are dwindling
You can see the levels fall
It's no good robbing Peter
Just to repay Paul

The gardens down in Melbourne
Are all beautiful and green
Ours is just a dustbowl
Not what they could have been

We have to fix this problem
And increase the country's stock
Not listen to the politicians
Who just go off ad hoc

Australia has plenty of water
But the problem that we face
Is making sure that water
Is used in just the right place

I know it's only a short solution
But before we go insane
Perhaps we should get an Indian
To do his dance for rain

Bottoms Up

Attention ladies and gentlemen
I'd like to call a toast
Would you all please raise your glasses
To the people I love most

Would you please raise up your glasses
To my dearest darling wife
Who encourages me to do my thing
And just enjoy my life

Would you all take another sip
To the family I adore
Who always help me if I'm down
And lift me from the floor

Another sip to my mother-in-law
Who's been very good to me
She's a lady who's loved by all
That's very plain to see

And to all my other in-laws
And extended family
Who welcomed me into their lives
That's as good as it can be

Would you please bend your elbows
To my brothers overseas
I wish we could meet more often
But that's not meant to be

Drink a drop to my mum and dad
Whose lives have long since passed
My dad died fighting in the war
And my mum was just a blast

Now drink a toast to the friends I've made
And the ones that I still know
And to all you people reading this
My friendly feelings flow

There's one more toast I'd like to make
Inside these friendly walls
Would you please raise up your glasses
To my bag of bowling balls

Power to the People

Are you friendly with your neighbours?
Do you chat across the fence?
Or do you just ignore them
Are the problems too immense

If you multiply your problems
By a million fold or more
That's what it's like here on earth
You'd never keep the score

We've got terrorists and bombers
Dictators and despots
Trying to do their damnest
To ruin what we've got

We don't try to ruin any country
Or tell them how to pray
Why not sit around a table
Let everyone have their say

Millions of people homeless
Children starve each day
While some dirty rotten scoundrel
Takes their livelihood away

We've had lots and lots of wars
Trying to find a cure
Do we leave it to the politicians?
Their lives are not that pure

We have to find some statesmen
Who'll stand for up for us and try
To attempt to find some common ground
The flag of peace to fly

Guns are not the answer
Our voices must be heard
There's nothing that's as powerful
As the people's spoken word

The Rookie Policeman

I want to be a policeman
To be a rookie cop
They sent me out to the Academy
To learn to make the traffic stop

They put me at a traffic light
To help the traffic flow
But I caused a lot of pileups
I didn't know that green meant go

The sergeant said you stupid sod
I'm putting you on the beat
So I put on my uniform
And boy did I look neat

I first arrested one guy
Breaking into a shop
In court he said I'm the owner
He was only locking up

Then I caught a prostitute
Trying to ply her trade
But she was an undercover cop
Taking part in a drug bust raid

So then it's off to the firing range
To learn to fire a gun
I was only there a little while
I accidently shot someone

They tried me as a detective
Snazzy suit and wide brimmed hat
I fell off a roof while giving chase
So that put an end to that

I got a driving licence
To drive the Divvy Van
I ran over a bloke on crutches
I'm doing the best I can

They transferred me to the local school
Gave me a bucket and mop
Told me in my spare time
I could hold the lollypop

It didn't take long to muck that up
I tried my heart and soul
Now I'm gardening at the station
Working for the Dole

The Milkman

The milkman delivers in our area
He goes from house to house
He delivers in the nighttime
But as quietly as a mouse

If you want to change your order
Just leave him out a note
Then he leaves the extra milk there
That he carries on his float

He comes round once a fortnight
Always the same day
But some of the doors he knocks on
He gets paid a different way

This man is a handsome devil
Always full of charm
However he gets his payments
He doesn't do much harm

Always good to little kids
He lets them ride upon his float
Keeps lots and lots of different sweets
In the pockets of his coat

Then one day a mistake was made
In a house collecting his bill
When the husband walked in through the door
I can hear the yelling still

I didn't know she was married
I heard the milkman shout
Get down on your knees, the husband said
It's time for me to knock you out

The door came flying open
Which man was the best
But I quickly came to realise
He's the fastest milkman in the west

The Fisherman

Our fishermen live a dangerous life
Out on the stormy sea
Trying to catch that elusive fish
For the likes of you and me

Their job is fraught with danger
When by the sea they're tossed
Sometimes giving up their lives
Is the fish really worth the cost?

They battle with the elements
As the heavy net they haul
And when they're waiting for the next
It's into the cot they crawl

But it's not just the sea they fight
It's wind and lashing rain
Working on the rain soaked deck
Ready to haul again

They fish out there for days on end
Their captain takes the lead
To fill the holds with shining fish
To satisfy our greed

But can the oceans continue
To sustain the fish we take
Or is there some alternative
We may be forced to make

But the fisherman continue
To satisfy our yearning
To put their lives at risk once more
For the money that they're earning

So when we go out shopping
For our seafood barbecue
Do we think of their frost bitten fingers?
I'll leave that thought with you

The Restaurant Nightmare

Have you been out to dinner
To a local restaurant
The waiter gives you a menu
But you don't know what you want

He stands there huffing and puffing
While he stares up at the roof
The waiter is an idiot
And you won't want too much proof

You finally make your mind up
And tell him what you chose
But he says that's off the menu
He's a waiter "You Suppose"

But you want to impress your partner
So persevere with him
Try and show some patience
He can't be all that dim

He suggests the head chef's special
An entree and a main
But he brings the main to the table first
This man must be insane

You decide to give it one more try
Say you'd like the entrees first
He asks you if you're ordering wine
Because you're working up a thirst

You ask for a bottle of chardonnay
But soon you shake your head
This stupid idiot waiter
Has brought a bottle of red

Your patience is exhausted
You know you've had enough
You've tried to impress your partner
This night's been really rough

You tell him he's been terrible
But he doesn't give a toss
He doesn't know you own the restaurant
And you really are his boss

You tell him who you really are
But he gives a kind of smirk
Then he's at the CES
'Cos now he's out of work

The Circus

I love to go to the circus
To see the animals there
See the artists on the trapeze
Go tumbling through the air

The clowns come running in
The fun when they perform
One gets drenched with water
And sits there all forlorn

With baggy pants and painted faces
Great big shoes upon their feet
With funny cars and slapstick
They make the night complete

Then in come the elephants
Answering their trainer's call
Standing up on hind legs
And balancing a ball

Next come the horses
Beautiful in step
The riders doing bareback tricks
They are the best ones yet

After that the lions come in
Inside a huge steel cage
The trainer cracks his whip at them
And the lions become enraged

The whip he holds in one hand
A chair is in the other
The lions leap across the cage
While we let go a shudder

Soon we see the jugglers
And a man that's breathing fire
Then we have to hold our breath
At the man up on the wire

The evening's been fantastic
Our hearts have beaten faster
All controlled by the man in red
That wonderful ringmaster

The Club

If you're a member of a club
It's to enjoy your life
Not stir up lots of trouble
And give other members strife

It's good to make suggestions
But you don't always get your way
You have to make allowances
For what other people say

None of us are perfect
And we're never always right
Sometimes it pays to listen
And keep your mouth shut tight

When you're the Chairman of a meeting
Do the others get a choice
Or are they forced to sit and listen
To the sound of just your voice

Do you think because you're chairman
That you are never wrong
Do you always want to get your way
And make the others play along

As a member it's your duty
Do nothing they resent
Be honest in your endeavours
Of the men you represent

And if you're not the chairman
Just a member of the board
Keep an eye on how things go
And make sure there's accord

Boxing

Do you think that boxing is a cruel sport?
When they stand there toe to toe
Trying to beat the crap
From an opponent that they don't know

They train so hard for months on end
So they can show some class
Then maybe box for just one round
And end up on their arse

The trainer says a left jab
Then cross it with your right
Your opponent ducks right under them
And then puts out your lights

You go back to work on Monday
Two beautiful black eyes
Start training for your next fight
Do you think that's really wise?

You've been very lucky lately
And won a fight or two
You're fighting for the Championship
Now who's the favourite? You

When you train you pound the pavement
And you use the skipping rope
You build your muscles with the weights
You are The Great White Hope

Now you're at the weigh in
You're heavier than him
But both are under the limit
And your trainer gives a grin

He gives you your instructions
To Bob and Weave and Dance
He is the heavier puncher
So don't give him a chance

The Fight goes all the fifteen rounds
You're still up on your toes
You land a flurry of punches
He must be glad, the bell goes

It seems you've won the fight on points
You can hear the crowd all scream
Suddenly the screaming stops
Another bloody dream

Cleaning Windows

I thought I'd clean some windows
To earn some extra dough
It didn't matter how high they were
Up the ladder I would go

I collected all the equipment
Canvassed the neighbourhood
Gave them all cheap prices
And a promise I'd be good

The day dawned bright and clear
I'd go to my first job
But put the ladder through the window
The repairs would cost a bob

My next job is a high one
My heart is all a flutter
The ladder slips, my feet come off
And I'm hanging on the gutter

The gutter gave way and down I go
I really don't know how far
Then I hear an awful crash
I've landed on a car

Very slow I pick myself up
Things couldn't get any worse
There's a hell of a lot of shouting
And I heard the owner curse

I hope you've got insurance
That's a very expensive car
And if you haven't got insurance
You are a bloody galah

I thought I'd give it one more go
To try and earn some money
But I broke two plate glass windows
This job is no longer funny

What else is going to happen
What else can I do wrong
What else will I stuff up
My will power's not that strong

I just wanted to make some money
With a ladder and a pail
I've damaged so much property
I'm writing this from jail

It's Time

Have you ever sat in a quiet room
Just listening to the clock
Hoping for a visitor
But no one comes to knock

We use the clock for many things
Not just for telling time
We check to see if something's cooked
That's how I use mine

If you're an athlete breaking records
And although you know you've won
Did you cover the distance quicker
Than some other runners run

Some clocks just make ticking sounds
Others have lovely chimes
The pendulum swings back and forth
I don't know how many times

Have you seen that clock up on the wall
There's a bird locked up inside
Comes flying out, says cuckoo
Then goes back and hides

There's a grandfather clock higher than me
That stands out in the hall
It seems to stand there like a sentry
Why are they made so tall?

There's a clock in the bedroom
And I know nobody cares
But when you set the alarm it sits there
It's silent, malignant, just stares

If you have to get up early one morning
The alarm you'll have to set
You didn't switch it on, it didn't go off
It's something you'll always regret

The chimes we hear on the radio
Is a clock that's called Big Ben
A sound we hear around the world
Again and again and again

But as people we want convenience
So we made a clock with a twist
We made it small and with a strap
Then we fixed it to our wrist

Flight Through the Ages

The hot-air balloon was the first
To rise above the ground
They lit a fire beneath a bag
Above a basket that was round

The Wright brothers made an aeroplane
That flew a little way
The doubters of a serious flight
Had nothing left to say

Tri-planes became bi-planes
And then the single wing
Propellers more efficient
Engines began to sing

Soon it had to happen
Passengers in flight
Aeroplanes with closed in sides
It was an awesome sight

The jet engine was born
Only because of war
They had to beat the enemy
And even up the score

Demand meant spending money
The public wanted more
To fly with other passengers
Out to a foreign shore

Bigger planes were needed
With Boeing on the scene
Planes would carry hundreds
Technology went green

The English and French built Concord
Flies above the speed of sound
The fastest passenger plane ever built
Now that one's not around

Now there are some aeroplanes
That are two stories high
With six hundred passengers
It's a wonder they can fly

A Real Policeman

Would you want to be a policeman
We curse them all the time
Their lives revolve around trouble
Drunks and drugs and crime

They have to deal with everything
Not much chance for smiles
With blood and death from accidents
And those sickening paedophiles

They don't just arrest a drunk
And keep him for the night
There might be a murder in your town
A riot or a gang war fight

Would you like to go to an overdose?
Or attend a suicide
It's sometimes quite a gruesome job
There's nowhere they can hide

The telephone rings and they're on call
Not knowing what they'll see
Their working life is making it safe
For the likes of you and me

Finding buried bodies
People who have drowned
All they see is heartbreak
It goes on all year round

If you get a speeding ticket
Were you driving much too fast
Can you blame him when he stops you?
Too late! The die was cast

Imagine what it would be like
If the Police were never seen
The criminal element would take over
And chaos reign supreme

We appreciate the police force
For all the work you do
The thousands of your members
Our safety's thanks to you

Would you want to be a policeman
We curse them all the time
Could you do all the things I've mentioned
In this little thank you rhyme

Our Town

We came here quite a few years ago
To this lovely little town
On peoples faces you see smiles
There's just no need to frown

There's lots of things to do here
A fantastic place to shop
With cafes on the sidewalks
If you feel the need to stop

There's two fantastic chemists
Tattslotto, butchers and ladies shops galore
There's supermarkets and grog shops
Who could ask for anything more

There's a jeweller and paint shops
Hairdressers to make you look real smart
There's gift shops and furniture
And our post office is just a work of art

There's garages and restaurants
There's pubs and pokies too
Bowling clubs and a golf course
Everything for me and you

There's a caravan park and a toy shop
There's even KFC
There's fish and chips and McDonald's
It really is the place to be

There's bakeries and sports shops
Most of the banks are here
There's a craft shop and video hire
Is the picture getting clear

There's a newsagent and haberdashery
Florists and a two dollar shop
A marriage celebrant and a hospital
In fact we've got the lot

Our Friends the Locals

A man worked in his garden
Being very thorough
Above his head he heard a noise
It was the local kookaburra

He yelled get off with you
Go away, go on, shoo
When around the corner hopped
A big grey kangaroo

He said don't do that
The kookaburra is my friend
And so is that big koala
Sitting down the end

The koala said whatever you do
Don't just stand and stare
But look at that big brown wombat
Standing by your chair

The wombat slowly shook his head
And said how do you do?
Let me introduce you to
A golden crested cockatoo

The cockatoo squawked
Said I know where
I can see old man emu
Over there

They sat around a campfire
The kookaburra, koala and kangaroo
The wombat, emu
And golden crested cockatoo

They decided there and then
Many more friends they'd make
They didn't see the movement in the shadows
Of the five foot tiger snake

But they welcomed him into their circle
Said how many have we got?
Not many said the crocodile
As he ate the bloody lot

Our Garden

When we moved into our house
The garden was a mess
So we sat down and made a plan
Of the problems we'd address

We pulled out lots of bushes
Shrubs and even trees
Then we started on the lower stuff
Working on our knees

After digging in the fertiliser
And lots and lots of earth
We started planting roses
For all that we were worth

Some roses are called standards
Others are called tea
Some are floribunda
They're all beautiful to me

We've got agapanthus and petunias
Weeping cherry, irises and chrisanths
Everyone says how nice it looks
We can only just say thanks

We pulled up rocks and concrete
When we started out the back
We seem to be more organised
Perhaps we've got the knack

We've put in plum trees and apples
A peach and apricots
Nectarines and cherries
Of fruit, we should get lots

We wanted to have some vegies
Growing in our ground
And see the fruits of our labours
Now that we walk around

Gone Fishing

Have you ever fished the Murray
That mighty river of ours
Have you sat there waiting for a bite
For what seems like many hours

And when you finally get one
And catch that elusive fish
Is it just a big old carp
Not the cod that you had wished

Now if you light a campfire
Its safety please ensure
We all of us have seen what happens
And what our firemen must endure

But camping by the riverside
Is a pleasant thing to do
And if you catch a Murray cod
Then I say, lucky you

Now remember when you're camping
With all the things you take
Please leave the campsite as you found it
And not the mess some people make

But you're fishing from the riverbank
Much better than watching telly
When suddenly you land one
A great big yellow belly

The fishing's getting better now
You can feel them start to feed
And although you're catching plenty
Don't take more than you'll need

Now remember our environment
Think of future generations
They might want to fish in just your spot
They might be your relations

The Garbage Man

The man that collects our garbage
Really is a strange guy
He comes at 5:30 in the morning
I'm going to ask him why

He bangs and clangs the garbage bins
Makes sure we're all awake
I'll get up early one morning
And give him quite a shake

Then one morning it happened
He went to empty the bin
But he slipped over on the back step
And tipped it all over him

The driver got out to help him
But things went bad to worse
He slipped over in all the garbage
You should have heard him curse

They struggled to their feet
But the truck had rolled away
Things were getting grimmer
This is not a very good day

The truck hit all the garbage bins
With rubbish everywhere
They stood ankle deep in refuse
And could only stand and stare

A policeman arrived
Said what's going on
The driver said the brake slipped
I did nothing wrong

The policeman said there's a hell of a mess
That someone's got to clean
But both the garbage men took off
Never again to be seen

Cricket

There's lots and lots of cricket
So we can pick and choose
We can see the excitement of the winners
And the sadness when they lose

We can sit and watch a test match
That sometimes lasts five days
We can see Ponting score a century
And spinners trying different ways

We'd never miss watching Gilchrist
Our most exciting batsman ever
Clear the long on boundary
Would we miss that? No, never

Now we've got fifty over matches
With new rules and regulations
New young batsmen coming through
That are a revelation

We put new young blood with old heads
And top batsmen to the fore
Some men are mister excitement
There's never been men like that before

Whether he's scoring heaps of runs
Or doing his bowling stint
What he's worth to the Australian side
He must be worth a mint

Twenty twenty over matches
Are really quite brand new
The public seem to like them
Though there's only been a few

With Lee bowling thunderbolts
And Gilchrist taking catches
Ponting setting out his field
The wickets come in batches

Test matches for the purists
Fifty overs for the thrill
Twenty overs for excitement
But I love it, always will

The Pirate

The pirate captain wore a patch
That tied behind his head
As he stared down at his captives
They all were filled with dread

He said right you lot
You all are going to hang
Unless you join our motley crew
A member of our pirate gang

One of the prisoners standing there
Said I'm only four foot tall
But I will join your pirate crew
If you let me fire a cannon ball

The captain said you want to fire
Upon a sailing ship
So they shoved him down the cannons barrel
And then the fuse they lit

The cannon fired, the man came out
Up in to the air
He passed a seagull flying by
Did he give him a scare

The seagull dropped a little parcel
As he went flying by
The captain stood there looking up
And it landed in his eye

The man flew on at break neck speed
His flight not over yet
A lot of people got a shock
As he overtook a jumbo jet

The pilot said I'm flying
As fast as this plane can
I recognise that man out there
It's a four foot superman

The Wedding Blues

Have you ever been to a wedding
Where the bride's guests stand and stare
While the guests from the other side
Look back at them and glare

I know that this thing happens
More often than you think
I've seen some guests at weddings
Get drunk and cause a stink

They're standing at the alter
The vicar asks him for the ring
The best man searches though his suit
He's lost the bloody thing

The bride started crying
The bridegroom said be quiet
We'll just get a bit of wire
And round your finger tie it

They got to the reception
When pandemonium breaks out
There is no food and where's the band
The best man's fault, no doubt

The best man got up to make his speech
He said I'm telling you all right now
I know a bloke slept with the bride
She wasn't much good anyhow

It was then the big fight started
In-laws face to face
One threw a piece of wedding cake
And then said I'll say grace

The fathers were really at it
Trading blow for blow
One said you big fat slob
The bride's an ugly so and so

Then someone called out bridal waltz
Now that was a sight to see
The brides dress was torn in half
From her breast down to her knee

After that the police arrived
And took away the groom
The bride then said to his best man
Let's not waste a honeymoon

Racing Round the World

I'd love to drive a racing car
And tangle with the greats
Then see the look of envy
On the faces of my mates

I'm turning in to a corner
With another on my tail
He does all he can to pass me
But it's all to no avail

One car is up in front of me
As we race through the chicane
I almost lose it big time
I won't do that again

But I catch him on the corner
And slip up his inside
He tried to drive defensive
But there's nowhere he can hide

They've heard of my accomplishments
And offer formula one
I'm in a single seater
That's something I've not done

So here I am around the world
Driving for my fans
I feel that I'm so good at this
I could do it with no hands

They want me at Ferrari
At Sauber and Williams too
But I'm partners with another
Australian through and through

It's the last race of the season
I know I must succeed
If I'm to be world champion
And satisfy my need

I turn the final corner
I know I'm at the front
Someone hits me up the rear
And gives me quite a shunt

I fight the car, regain control
It's not as it would seem
Suddenly the alarm goes off
Another stupid dream

At the Park

I used to take the kids to the park
And push them on the swing
Hear their joyous shouts and laughter
As other kids joined in

They used to like the slippery slide
As they screamed and took their turn
A queue would form at the ladder
And don't push in, they'd learn

Then it was off to the round a bout
Hanging on real tight
Some of them screamed with enjoyment
Some of them with fright

They took turns on the seesaw
Up and down they'd go
With smiles upon their faces
I wished they'd never grow

I watched my laughing children
Who now had numbered four
I was the proudest parent
Perhaps we should have more

Then we'd get the gear out
Go on the grassy patch
Gather up the other kids
And have a cricket match

With the kids running everywhere
The fun you'd never match it
Someone hits it in the air
And the yell goes up to catch it

Now my kids are all grown up
With children of their own
They ask their kids to go to the park
But they only get a groan

They're playing on the computer
Or something called iPod
Go and play in the park Dad?
They couldn't give a sod

At the Funfair

The traveling fun fairs come to town
And we're all of us going to go
We'll try out all the amusements
And then see a funny show

First I'll try the rifle range
I was a pretty good shot
The man said I've won a prize
I can pick from what he's got

Next I tried the clowns
With open mouth and turning head
But I wasn't very good at that
I think that's what he said

I wanted to try the tin cans
Standing in a pile
I threw the balls as hard as I could
But missed them by a mile

My girlfriend wanted fairy-floss
I said that that's ok
You can have whatever you want
We gonna enjoy this day

Have you tried the bows and arrows
The arrows are all bent
No matter where you aim them
That's never where they went

Then I tried the darts
And won a prize from that
I told my girlfriend she could choose
And she chose a furry cat

We went to see the bearded lady
Thought that was pretty grim
I don't think that the beard was real
And it cost a dollar to get in

I tried to be a show-off
And ring that bell up there
Three goes for fifty cents
But I don't really care

We'd spent a lovely day there
My girlfriend gave a smile
Said let's go back to my place
Parents won't be home for quite a while

Fairies in the Garden

There are fairies in our garden
I often hear them sing
In the morning I go down
To try and find their fairy ring

Last night I crept into the garden
To try and see them there
I knew I mustn't disturb them
I knew I mustn't dare

It must have been a special night
There were hundreds dancing there
Some were dancing round in circles
Others hovering in the air

Suddenly a special one appeared
Her aura coloured gold
I tried to get a little closer
But not to be too bold

She hovered there in a shining light
I think she was the Queen
The most beautiful little creature
That I have ever seen

They held a kind of ceremony
I just don't know what for
The Queen was very much in charge
Her word it seemed was law

I knew they mustn't see me
I didn't know what they'd do
I'd try and come another night
Our acquaintance to renew

Are there fairies in your garden
Do you ever hear them sing
In the morning do you go down
And try to find their fairy ring

Are You Feeling Fruity

If you would eat an apple
Every single day
They taste all crunchy in your mouth
And your bowels will be ok

I like to eat a pear
Right after morning tea
They help to keep me healthy
And taste quite good to me

Apricots are funny fruit
They taste better off by far
If you spread them on your morning toast
When you get them from a jar

Do you like a juicy cherry
Or a really succulent peach
Can you stand beneath the fruit tree
And eat what you can reach

What about an orange
Or a juicy piece of melon
But do you really screw your face up
If you try to eat a lemon

Have you ever eaten tangerine
And then got lots of pips
You work them round inside your mouth
Then blow them through your lips

Would you like a nectarine
Every single day
But any fruit is healthy
That's what the doctors say

Now what about the strawberry
They make a lovely scene
When you've got them in a bowl
Covered in thick whipped cream

But I must admit my favourite
Is the juicy old blood plum
I think that they're the greatest
They're just the best bar none

Nervous in the Night

Have you ever seen a ghost?
Or a misty apparition
Have you felt there's something there?
Just a feeling or suspicion

Do you ever feel a shiver?
Go over you like a wave
They say it's caused by someone
Walking on your grave

You feel that someone's watching
But there's no-one in the room
When you're nervous in the dark
You know you're not immune

Have you ever heard strange footsteps?
Walking down the hall
You quickly open up the door
But there's no-one there at all

Do you wake up in the night?
Think someone's standing there
Have you seen a strange old lady?
In a strange old rocking chair

Did you hear strange rattling noises?
From underneath the floor
Perhaps someone is buried there
That lived in the house before

Have you walked into your kitchen?
The place is just a mess
Perhaps it was a poltergeist
But you can only guess

There's a dark and empty mansion
Forbidding in the night
A shadow moves in the window
That's lit by candlelight

You're walking past a cemetery
There's something in there, white
Is that a movement in the shadows?
Did a noise give you a fright?

You must release your emotions
Your fear of the dark won't last
The bedroom door is open
Did I see a ghost go past?

Our Wild World

They say the earth is very old
Millions and millions of years
Yet still we're lashed by the wind and storms
That justify our fears

While the earth turns on its axis
Cyclonic storms are forming
They come tearing down upon our towns
With very little warning

We have volcanoes spewing lava
In what's called the ring of fire
With townships near the mountains
Their consequences dire

Earthquakes are a problem
They come at any time
They shake the land we walk on
No warning and no sign

Some earthquakes that occur
Happen out at sea
Causing giant tsunamis
Destroying communities

When an earthquake happens near a city
Dam walls come tumbling down
The water rushes down upon them
And many people drown

Buildings collapse and fires rage
And services are destroyed
Then for months on end thereafter
It's a place we all avoid

With the storms and lashing rain
Many homes are lost
There goes workers' livelihoods
And the people bear the cost

Think of the world around us
And what can happen there
Of the disasters that we live with
And the problems we all bear

But most of us are lucky
We live safe and sound
So try and help your neighbours
When disaster comes to town

Weapons of the Ages

We started off by throwing rocks
To try and kill some game
It didn't matter what we got
It didn't have a name

Then we got quite clever
And fashioned wooden spears
We then took on much larger game
Surround them with our peers

Soon we had some sharp edged flint
To tie on to the end
We learnt to attack our neighbours
And how to defend

Later on came hardened steel
We learnt to make a hatchet
Those with only stone edged weapons
We knew we'd never match it

Someone made a bow and arrow
We could kill from far away
This was our greatest weapon yet
I think that's fair to say

With bows and arrows and metal spears
We started making war
They didn't think where we were headed
No one ever saw

Suddenly the gun was born
We could kill and kill some more
At first our fights were local
Now it's international war

After guns came bombs and shells
Then rockets reigned supreme
We could kill them without leaving home
Much better it would seem

The strongest ruled the weak
Diplomacy of the gun
You do all we ask of you
Or we kill everyone

Then one day a bomb was made
That could kill us all we know
Perhaps we should never have found that rock
We should never have learnt to throw

The Milky Way

Do you sit and watch the sky
On a still and cloudless night
And look up at the stars
All glittering and bright

Can you see the Southern Cross
That's on our national banner
Can you see our neighbouring planets
With a telescope or scanner

We're in a huge great galaxy
That's called the Milky Way
And ever since our time began
It's always been that way

Remember as a child
You liked to join the dots
If you tried it with the stars
Of shapes you would get lots

Can you make a frying pan
Can you make a great big bear
You really can have endless fun
Joining them up there

Did you see Halley's Comet
When it was flying by
With its long and fiery tail
As it streaked across the sky

If you could ride a rocket
Way up into space
You'd see asteroids and meteors
As across our sky they'd race

Why do some stars twinkle
And others they just shine
I don't know the answer
Perhaps I will in time

Of the millions of stars in the heavens
Our Earth is just one dot
It's impossible to count them
There really is a lot

Men work giant telescopes
That search amongst the stars
Trying to find a similar world
Millions of miles past Mars

In the Army

Our man joined the army
And we know that he's not tall
They wouldn't let him play football
'Cos he'd never pass the ball

When he put on his uniform
The trousers were too long
The jacket came down to his knees
Everything looked wrong

They gave him a great big kit bag
It was long and it was round
But when he put his stuff in it
He couldn't lift it off the ground

Right, they said, we're going on a march
Up the mountain track
But when the Sargent looked behind him
Our man was two miles further back

They asked him would he like to drive
A tank with a great big gun
But when they tried to get a crew for him
A stranger was the only one

They're out there on manoeuvres
Our man said the barrel's bent
'Cos we've just hit the colonels jeep
And arse over tip he went

The army sent them overseas
The enemy to fight
But when they reached the battlefront
Our man said it's not right

So he telephoned the enemy
And said, I'm sure we've got the time
Let's have a chat over a cup of tea
Or perhaps a glass of wine

The army said we're in a war
Not over here to talk
So our man dropped his bottom lip
And went off for a power walk

So our man retired to Australia
Not making any noise
He sits there quietly waiting
Will he get a job for the boys

Waterfalls

I love to sit near a waterfall
And see the raging torrent
Forget the worries of the world
Which really are abhorrent

I'd like to stand behind the water
Falling like a curtain
What a fantastic thing to see
Of that, I would be certain

The salmon like to leap up some
To get to their spawning ground
But hunters are waiting at the top
With great big bears all around

Usually they are quite a walk
Can't go by car to many
With my approaching senior years
I soon won't visit any

Right now I think it's beautiful
Just to watch and listen
See the water droplets in the air
As they fall they shine and glisten

Some waterfalls are not that big
And some are very high
It's dangerous to swim beneath
You're foolish if you try

You see birds flying from the mist
Catching insects on the wing
It's all part of the ecosystem
When waterfalls just do their thing

But I just like to sit and listen
As they roar down from above
I haven't got a favourite one
It's all of them I love

Our Four Legged Friends

If you want to get yourself a dog
Which one would you choose
A tiny wee Chihuahua
Or a Great Dane you can't lose

You could have a Pekinese, schnauzer or kelpie
A Rottweiler terrier or Dalmatian
What about a boxer, greyhound or a whippet
A spaniel, bulldog or Alsatian

What's better than a bloodhound or St Bernard
For when you're lost in snow
Or a coiffured standard poodle
If you want to win a show

There's a pointer, wolfhound or Staffy
Jack Russell, border collie or chow
A Pomeranian, dingo or a ridgeback
But don't choose one just now

Pick a Maltese shiatsu, or dachshund
These dogs are only small
You could choose a healer, husky or retriever
Now those are fairly tall

I wouldn't pick a pit bull
They're nasty and they bite
But a lovely little beagle
I'm sure that they're all right

I don't think that the wolf is one
That you're allowed to keep
Red setter is a nice one
But they just like to sleep

There's not many left to choose from
But the golden Labrador
And the rough and ready mongrel
You'll love forever more

I hope this list has helped you
To know just where you're at
And if you can't make a choice from here
Then you better get a cat

Who is Watching Who

Do you sit and watch your television
Are your eyes still round, or square
Can you think of anything better to do
Than sit around and stare

The programs that they put on
That they want us to see
Are filled up with advertisements
Unless we watch the ABC

I think plastic people live inside
And they speak the scripted word
And the situations that they live in
Are really quite absurd

There's a lot of sport on telly
And you can watch the horses race
And are you sick of all the reruns
That should never be the case

It's American cops and robbers
Or English comedy
But where's the Aussie programs
That I would like to see

We used to get In Melbourne Tonight
With Grahame and Burt, so funny
But now the TV stations
Are just concerned with making money

Chanel 7 does Tattslotto
It used to be at half past eight
Now when you want the numbers
They could be forty minutes late

Do you sit and watch your television
Is your life really such a bore
I'll give you one suggestion
You really should go out some more

Clouds

You should sit and watch the clouds
As they float across the sky
I often sit and wonder
How can they fly so high

I sit and watch the cumulus
Rounded masses, pearly white
Making faces at the edges
I sometimes do all right

You can't do much with stratus clouds
They're just continuous and flat
They make the days look miserable
I'm not too pleased with that

Cirrus clouds are woolly filaments
Shapely changing as they move
Making pretty patterns in the sky
I'm sure you would approve

Now nimbus clouds are different
They're dark and full of rain
You sometimes see the lightning
When thunder booms again

We know the farmers need the rain
But not a huge great flood
That tends to turn their farmland
To a great big sea of mud

They sometimes give us hailstones
As big as a tennis ball
Causing lots of damage
We don't need those at all

But nimbus clouds do give us
Steady soaking rain
Good for our environment
We hope they come again

I know we need these clouds
They're good for everyone
Don't need them at the beach though
'Cos they block out all the sun

Moomba

Have you ever been to Moomba?
On the Labour Day weekend
Seen the skiers on the Yarra
Come flying round the bend

Have you stood up in the city?
Seen the floats go down the street
Clapped your hands at the marching bands
As they march to their own beat

Have you been out to the funfair?
Bought the kids their fairy floss
Glad you've got the day off
Away for the day from the boss

Have you ridden on some rides?
Brought your heart up to your throat
Been on the one goes back and forth
Like you're on a great big boat

It all costs a lot of money
You're glad it's just one day
As the kids will keep on asking
Just one more ride Dad eh?

I must admit my favourite
Is just sitting on the grass
Watching those daring skiers
As they go flying past

The tricks they do are marvellous
And it's all done on one ski
Sometimes they crash in the water
I'm where I'd rather be

When they do the slalom
Keep shortening the rope
Trying to beat the others
At least that's what they hope

But what about the spectacle
As they soar high off the jump
They land back in water
And then their fist they pump

But we should thank the workers
For this holiday that's set
To celebrate the Eight Hour Day
They fought so hard to get

The Lady Driver

The lady driver is a problem
You can hear the men all say
They never indicate when they're turning
And they're always in the way

They do forty when it's sixty
About as fast as men can walk
A fag hanging from their mouth
And on their mobiles talk

They don't know where reverse is
When parking space they spot
They'll leave it in the invalid's place
They do that quite a lot

They go flying down the freeway
Foot down to the floor
Pulled over by a policeman
The tears start to pour

They say they didn't mean it
They don't like to go that fast
The policeman gives a smirk and grunts
And then gives her a blast

They never have an accident
Although they cause a few
And they're always driving great big cars
That seem to be brand new

You can always hear them coming
The radio up loud
You can always pick a woman driver
She stands out from the crowd

But wait! I've got this poem all mixed up
It's male drivers that I mean
I hope I've not upset the women
As I exit from the scene

The Indian

The Indians live in tepees
And I really shouldn't jest
In places like Colorado
Or out in America's west

They walk around in war paint
Saying Ugh and you white man
They act like they are warriors
Even on the tram

They ride their painted ponies
And when they die, they moan
Then when the filming's over
It's in the car, and home

But there really were some shockers
Like in Custer's Own Last Stand
When Chief Sitting Bull scalped him
Down to his last strand

He waved the scalp around him
For all his men to see
But he took it from the wrong place
Two foot above the knee

The American government worried
And with some consternation
The Indians are walking
Off their reservation

They said they wanted blankets
And what made the country shocked
When they reported to the government
Their sewerage pipes were blocked

The cowboys don't go near them now
And the Indians don't worry
And what keeps everyone away
The strong smell of their curry

Spencer Street Station

I sat on the seat at Spencer Street
To watch the people pass by
I laughed at the things I saw there
I'll try and tell you why

Along came a bloke with a wooden leg
And he caught it in a grate
Someone said can I help you
Have you got a saw on you mate

They cut off the bit that jammed
And he limped off to the train
Everyone just laughed at him
He won't get it jammed again

A porter stood there in his uniform
His face was really smug
He swaggered up to a tattooed man
I thought it was a thug

The porter smiled and called him sir
And said can I help you mate
The tattooed man wanted to know
If his train left from this gate

The porter laughed and said it does
But you've been rather slow
You should have got here sooner
That train left an hour ago

Then a blonde walked by with five inch heals
And legs that went so high
Three men walked off the platform
And their wives just wondered why

Then I saw a drunken man
His legs wouldn't obey his brain
He kept on falling over
But he always got up again

He tried to get a ticket
From a machine standing there
He couldn't remember his destination
But he didn't really care

Suddenly his train arrived
And he climbed up on the step
Does this train go to Spencer Street
And the porter said you bet

Football

Do you like to watch the football
Have you got a special team
Do you pray to win a premiership
That really is a dream

Remember watching Ablett
Take a specky in the ground
Do you recall young Bartlett
Best crumber going round

Shinboner of the century
Glen Archer played it tough
And when your team is beaten
The umpiring was rough

Do you follow Essendon
A bomber through and through
Or are the Cats your favourite team
I say good luck to you

Maybe you cheer the Eagles
From way out in the west
Or maybe you support Fremantle
I don't know which one is best

Some follow the Bulldogs
Or good old Collingwood
If you don't follow the Magpies
You hate them, or you should

There's Sydney Swans and Brisbane
Port Adelaide and the Crows
I hope there's some supporters
For any one of those

Do you follow the mighty Hawks
Or Melbourne down in town
Perhaps your team's St Kilda
Who've only won one crown

I have to mention Tony Lockett
With the greatest score of all
But there were many other players
Who were better with the ball

Remember Jesaulenko
Fly up in the sky
I bet Jenkin still remembers
And he still remembers why

I haven't forgotten the Richmond club
I wouldn't leave them out
I've left till last the greatest club
It's Carlton without doubt

The Submarine

Wartime in a submarine
Is a dangerous place to be
Trying to catch an enemy ship
Rather him than me

But if you are discovered
Depth charges start to drop
You hope that there's no damage
From that war ship up on top

You very quietly make your escape
As you safely slip away
You are now a danger to the surface ships
With torpedoes ready for the fray

Up goes the periscope
An enemy in full view
You fire off two torpedoes
That is what submariners do

You watch the slowly sinking ship
And surface to make sure
You pick up any survivors
Prison life they must endure

Life goes on dealing death
To all that come in sight
Many ships get to know
The strength of a torpedoes bite

The war continues, when will it end
Then suddenly it does
You take the sub to the surface
The crew are all abuzz

Now you're sitting on the patio
Relaxed in Granddads rocker
You're sad for all the men that are
In Davy Jones' Locker

Dangers in the Oceans

There are dangers when you're out at sea
Where wind makes mountainous waves
Crashing down on fishing fleets
Driving sailors to their graves

Other dangers out at sea
Are the creatures living there
Some are small but dangerous
So everyone take care

The surfers are courageous
Riding those huge waves
They come out from those tunnels
Like emerging from a cave

But there are others lurking in the water
They swim just out of sight
Suddenly they flash towards you
You must evade their bite

Then there's the blue ringed octopus
Stay away, don't take a chance
One touch from those tentacles
And you're in the ambulance

There are some kinds of jellyfish
That float and never tire
One touch from their trailing tails
And your skin is just on fire

But the oceans are so beautiful
A playground for us all
Make sure you swim between the flags
Where lifeguards are on call

In the Navy

I know a man joined the navy
He thought that would be a ball
So when war was declared with Tasmania
He answered his country's call

The captain said you're a gunner
It won't take long to learn
That's your gun, right back there
The big one on the stern

Suddenly the alarm went off
The enemy's in sight
Man the guns you ugly lot
We'll give them all a fright

The Tasman ferry was bearing
Right across their bow
Sink it, yelled the captain
I really don't care how

So he fired his great big gun
And chaos reined supreme
The captain shouted stupid sod
You've sunk our submarine

The captain said, you're not a gunner
I'll just make you the cook
But by the end of the week he was sorry
'Cos most of the crew were crook

But our man got lots of medals
Because he had to make amends
And the reason he got so many
Is 'cos he stole them from his friends

But he will go down in history
When he went to war for Australia
The only time we were beaten
And that was by Tasmania

The Tractors

Now a man worked in Melbourne
For a firm he thought he'd stay
From the first day that he started
His boss regretted that day

The firm made mainly tractors
For working on the farm
Our man worked on the assembly line
Where he couldn't do much harm

Then it started happening
With tractors breaking down
And farmers getting angry
When they couldn't plough their ground

One farmer climbed on his tractor
You should have heard him curse
Instead of going forward
The thing went in reverse

The firm was really in trouble
And the men were all in strife
For not only did it go backwards
He ran over his neighbour's wife

The boss called our man to his office
Said I'm not going to give you the sack
But when you go home on Friday
For god sake don't come back

So our man moved to the country
Well he had to get out of town
When he heard one farmers tractor
Had drove in the lake and he drowned

So our man now lives amongst us
And there's one comment I will make
Don't let him fix your tractor
You might end up in the lake

The Cowboy

He rode into town
His six-gun tied down tight
He wanted to be successful
For the day to turn out right

He tied his horse outside
A place called the Silver Moon
He knew his quarry would be inside
This town only had one saloon

He walked in through the batwing doors
Saw his target at the bar
After eight long years of searching
Twenty feet is not too far

He yelled, your gang killed my parents
My sister, father and mother
I've caught up with all the rest
You're the last one left, my brother

I'm the twelve year old you left behind
Hiding behind the shed
Now you'll pay for what I lost
I'm going to shoot you, dead

They both went for their six-guns
Both men very fast
But the villains' gun never cleared its holster
When he heard the other gun blast

The witnesses said the fight was fair
As he gave his dying breath
The cowboy rode away that day
He'd avenged his families' death

The Photo (Part 1)

I was born in the town of Ramsgate
On England's southern coast
Of all the places that I've lived
It's the place I think of most

I started life in Leopold Street
Then moved to Dundonald Road
There we lived the war out
It was our safe abode

My brother and sister were evacuated
Up to a Staffordshire farm
They stayed there 'til the war ended
Out of the bombers harm

My Father was a paratrooper
He landed in a town in France
But the odds were overwhelming
My Dad never stood a chance

Always when the bombers came
Our sirens loudly blared
My Mum and I headed for the tunnels
Which our neighbours safely shared

The tunnels saved countless lives
And I'm sure everyone agreed
That our Mayor did a wonderful job
When he envisaged what we'd need

One day someone took a photo
Of a woman and her son
They put that photo in a book
And gave one to my Mum

It's sad to say the book got lost
When it was in my care
I was a married man with children then
And we searched everywhere...

The book is quite important
It shows me who I am
Because I'm the boy in the photo
I'd love to find it if I can

However, I found a copy
In London's *Daily Mail*
It hangs now in my hallway
Mum and me in the war in every single detail

To come and visit Ramsgate
Tops my Bucket List
It's everything I've hoped for
And everything I've wished

We'll make some new arrangements
Once this virus ends
Fulfil all our promises
And try to make amends

Now to end this little poem
There's one more thing to say
Look out Phil we're coming
And we'll soon be on our way

*...many thanks for the help and advice
from the tunnel committee, hoping you
remain healthy and strong*
K

The Following Years (Part 2)

Well the war is over now
It's time to celebrate
England's one big party
Ain't life really great

But some folks don't really party
It all seems rather sad
Probably they're just like me
In the war they lost their Dad

But life is getting better
Although our Mums still have to queue
Ready with their ration cards
To get supplies for me and you

A couple of years, Mum remarried
It helped to ease her load
My brother joined the Royal Marines
And I went to St Marys Road

When I started at St Marys
I was the cleverest kid in school
My Mum had taught me to be the best
That was her golden rule

She taught me to say the alphabet
Backwards, if you please
I could count up to fifty
I even learnt to read

At eleven I passed a scholarship
And went to Grammar School
But I wasn't really clever there
So I just played the fool

I hated that rich kids' place
For four long desperate years
Played truant as often as I could
And bought my Mum to tears

Eventually at age fifteen
They said that I could leave
Go back to the school I came from
I left the teachers quite relieved

At Hollyfield I was smarter
And I didn't do too much
I often looked after classes
Loved everything I touched...

I found a job not far from home
Working at turning metal
But I didn't like it very much
I just couldn't seem to settle

So I thought I'd try something new
Working with timber might be good
I spent most of my life with timber
I found a trade I'd hoped I would

I'm pretty good at what I did
But I felt I needed change
For many years I went painting
The best I could arrange

Then it was suspended ceilings
Now that was really good
Plenty of girlfriends around the country
I did what any man would

...If I write another book, I'll continue with my story

Victoria's West

Have you travelled around Victoria
The country and the coast
I love driving round our great state
It's prettier than most

You leave the city of Melbourne
And head down to Geelong
You're on the Western Highway
So that won't take too long

Keep looking for the signpost
That says Great Ocean Road
The most scenic drive in the world
That's what I've been told

You start off at Torquay
Then Lorne and Apollo Bay
Make sure you stop to look around
You've really got all day

Keep on going through Wattle Hill
See the Twelve Apostles, Loch ard Gorge
Port Campbell, London Bridge
Then on to Warnambool

Drive on to see Port Fairy
Go right round Portland Bay
Have coffee in Mount Gambier
Just a little out your way

We're going to Mildura
But we go through Horsham first
Warracknabeal and Ouyen
You've driven up a thirst

You've reached the Mighty Murray
So stop a day or two
Take a ride on a paddleboat
They've got quite a few

Then follow the river to Robinvale
Make Swan Hill your next stop
Go and see the settlement
This town has got the lot

You're heading for Cohuna
But first go through Kerang
Then you'll have to stay in Echuca
A good motel if you can

Off we go to Bendigo
Then on to Ballarat
Turn left and head for Melbourne
Then suddenly you're back

Ned Kelly

Ned Kelly was a robber
Riding with his gang
Holding up banks and traders
Stealing when he can

He thought he'd fool the policeman
And wear a suit of tin
They won't be able to get me now
I'm disguised as a garbage bin

He was robbing a café one fine day
Wearing his suit of tin
An employee took his hat off
And tipped the rubbish in

Bugger this said Kelly
I'm going to rob the bank
But they'd locked the doors and windows
'Cos someone nearby smelt rank

But the policeman had a tacking dog
And followed the Kelly smell
They surrounded Ned at his hideout
Then one of them gave a yell

Righto Ned you're under arrest
But he gave a little grin
You don't scare me, Ned yelled back
I'm wearing my suit of tin

Right said Ned, I need a leek
Before we start to run
He took off his metal trousers
A bullet hit him in the bum

Christ said Ned, that bloody hurts
Grabbing hold of his bum
You better help me to my horse
I don't think I can run

Then Ned knew he couldn't escape
The police had put a block up
I'm supposed to be a clever man
What a bloody cock up

They took him to Old Melbourne jail
And no one thought it odd
When they found Ned Kelly guilty
And hung the bloody sod

South Africa

My wife and I went to Africa
To see my brother there
He lives in the city of Cape Town
It was quite an expensive fare

Cape Town sits in a horseshoe
With Table Mountain at the rear
False Bay is in the foreground
A beautiful place no fear

We went up Table Mountain
To see the view from there
You can go up in a cable car
Now that gives you a scare

We drove to Kruger National Park
To see animals in the wild
We saw massive herds of zebra
And huge baboons with child

We saw hippos in the rivers
And lions lazing in the sun
Huge great tusks on the elephants
And they scared everyone

The giraffes were quite magnificent
Strolling past the car
But the warthogs were just great to watch
My favourites by far

The rhinos had a habit
Of defecating in one spot
And the buffalo stood there saying
What big horns we've got

We never saw a leopard
They only hunt at night
We saw an elephant with one tusk
Now he gave us a fright

But with all the beauty that we saw there
You couldn't do the sums
Of the millions and millions of Africans
Living in the slums

The white man in South Africa
Is living pretty good
But the natives of the country
Have done the best they could

Let's Go Buy a Motor Car

So you wanna buy a motor car
And you wanna drive the best
You need to take some test drives
And relegate the rest

So let's go and try the Commodore
If your family's really huge
But don't listen to the salesman
He's full of subterfuge

Now let's try the Falcon
They're really big as well
Not much different from the Holden
As far as we can tell

We won't forget Toyota
There's big improvement there
And if you drive the sporty one
You will get lots of stares

You'll have to test the Magna
I'm told they're really good
But it won't be made in Australia
If you think your new car should

Can you afford a BMW
They really cost a lot
The car that you decide on
Depends on what you've got

You'll want to test Mercedes
They're right there at the top
You'll love the way they handle
They are my cream of the crop

You haven't tried Hyundai
Or a snazzy little Kia
They really are a nice car
They come from South Korea

Well you must have made your mind up
On what's your favourite car
But you're going to keep the farm ute
'Cos it was driven by your Pa

You've tried out all the new cars
And the price was not a factor
You might as well sell the ute
And drive the rotten tractor

The Farmyard

Have you ever looked upon a cow
And seen how big they are
They're very big said a little kid
As big as my Dad's car

Have you ever stroked a grazing sheep
Pushed your fingers through their wool
Kept one eye open on the gate
For the charging of the bull

Have you ever stood up near the pigs
'Cos I'm not too keen on those
When the aroma slowly reaches you
You wrinkle up your nose

Have you ever watched
A big old billy-goat
Forcing food as fast as he can
Down his big old throat

Have you ever fed the chooks
Scratching on the ground
Making sure there's enough
Seed to go around

Have you collected all the eggs
From boxes in the pen
Watching for the cockerel
Who scares you now and then

Have you ever seen the dog
Rounding up the flock
Making sure that none escape
The runaways he'll block

Well you've been all round the farmyard
And checked the animals out
But you'll need to spend a lot of time there
To know what farming's all about

Have you slipped over in the yard
And sat down in the poo
Has your mother ever said
In the shower you

Life on the Road

I thought we'd buy a caravan
So we could tour around
We couldn't afford a new one
Second is what we found

The salesman said you've got your van
But an annex would be good
You can sit outside and have your meals
Like all good caravaners would

Off we went towing our van
But we never got too far
We soon got a busted bearing
On the back wheel of our car

But pretty soon we're on our way
Then neither of us spoke
We heard a sort of clanging noise
The rotten tow-bar broke

We got that fixed though it cost a lot
So we thought we'd make some tea
But we didn't have any water
And no gas that I could see

I said we'd get more organised
And have a thorough check
No breaking down in the bush
And have many miles to trek

Now we're ready to start our trip
Victoria we'd go round
Then I know you won't believe it
The stupid car broke down

But eventually we found a beach
Just like we had planned
Then all our luck went sour again
We bogged it in the sand

I didn't think I could take much more
But we'd try Lake Eildon first
We only got about fifty miles
And our radiator burst

Left home over a week ago
Got less than a hundred miles
We burnt the caravan there and then
The first time that we'd smiled

Storms

Have you ever watched the clouds
As they float across the sky
Some are called nimbostratus
I really don't know why

Then there are the dark ones
Heavy and full of rain
They darken up the landscape
Will daylight come again

Suddenly there's thunder
Loud with so much noise
Scaring all the animals
And frightening girls and boys

Crack goes the lightning
Electricity in the air
Causing many bush fires
We all must now take care

Homes burnt down and cattle dead
Hundreds of wildlife has been lost
Our firemen put the fires out
And our farmers count the cost

Then suddenly all is clear
The storms and rain have gone
We all sit back and wonder
Will the storm return, how long

We look up in the sky
And everywhere is blue
You must feel very lucky
That all is well with you

But wait, what's that far away
Another cloud appears
Is this the start of another storm
To bring back all our fears

I BLOODY HOPE NOT

Sydney

A friend of ours went to Sydney
Said it was a bustling place
Nothing moves very slowly
Everyone seems to race

But ride by public transport
Ride the double decker train
Nothing you can lose by that
And everything to gain

Ride the buses, train or ferry
For twenty four hours, no more
It only costs a few dollars
And it's all within the law

She went to the casino
And won a little bit
But some of the paying customers
Just didn't know how to quit

There's rows and rows of pokies
Standing there in line
Waiting to put your money in
Time after time after time

The shopping there's fantastic
Great big shopping malls
Where you can buy lots of presents
So don't forget your pals

Ride the ferry across the harbour
Go to Taronga Park zoo
What a wonderful array of animals
Just waiting there for me and you

Now it's a marvellous place to visit
If you're from overseas
But remember Australian customs
You can't do as you please

Ladies of the Night

They start off under a streetlight
Or the doorway of a shop
Hoping that a car will pause
Then hope that it will stop

He winds down his window
And they negotiate a price
Most men are embarrassed
But some are really nice

She gets into his car
The price agreed, ok
They drive round to her flat
That's not too far away

He gets what he's agreed upon
Then leaves her with a smile
She says I hope to see you again
I really like your style

She wants to graduate to a brothel
You're licenced and all is proper
Security is tight there
He might even be a copper

The place is furnished beautifully
Everything is clean
You go for regular health checks
Soft music all serene

The customers are all well dressed
And welcomed by the female boss
They're allowed to choose the girl they want
At the price they pay, there'll be no loss

But drugs are in the equation
That keeps girls on the game
It all started so innocent
So who can anybody blame?

Port Douglas

We went on holiday to Port Douglas
And stayed in a huge resort
This fabulous place we stayed in
Was nothing like what we'd been taught

The swimming pool had a built in bar
You could swim up for a drink
From an ice cold beer in a long tall glass
Or a gin that's coloured pink

The town itself was fabulous
So much to see and do
You'll never regret going there
I'll make that bet with you

We sailed out to an island
Miles way out to sea
Went scuba diving in wetsuits
To a beautiful coral cay

The ship we sailed was huge
A hundred people or more
Turtles and great shoals of fish
Just some of the things we saw

We went on a cute little train
To see where the sugar grew
We spent the morning doing that
Then found more things we could do

I've never seen so many restaurants
Food from every nation
They made your taste buds suffer
From all kinds of temptation

I hope I've given you an insight
To that wonderful town up there
But don't go swimming in the sea
There's salt water crocodiles, take care

Cold Shower Anyone

I went to the bathroom this morning
I thought I'd take a shower
But half way through the water went cold
Someone had turned off the power

So I quickly dried and got dressed
And went to find the reason why
I slipped on the floor, hit my head
And saw every star in the sky

I woke up in a furious mood
How much more could I take
A bump on my head and sore ribs
And a really thumping headache

Now someone's going to suffer
If I can find out who
The day they turned my gas off
Is the day that they will rue

I went outside and saw some kids
But the horrible mood I'm in
I mustn't punish the wrong ones
That would be a terrible sin

Then I had an idea
There were men working close by
Could they have turned my gas off
I have to find out why

I rushed at them, acting tough
And said what you did wasn't right
I wished I hadn't raised my fists
The hospital said I never won the fight

Western Australia, it's a Long Way

Have you ever travelled to Western Australia
It really is so far away
You drive across the Nullarbor Plain
Not a place you'd want to stay

It really is exciting
To take that great long drive
But watch out for the roadtrains
You need to stay alive

But do branch off that long straight road
To see the Australian Bight
Watch the whales with their young swim by
A most exciting sight

It really is a most wonderful place
A place that's like no other
But don't go on your own though
Take your wife, your sister or mother

You see all the animals on that drive
Some you've never seen
You pass a mob of kangaroos
And wonder where they've been

If you go at the right time of the year
You'll see all the wildflowers bloom
Like a carpet on the landscape
There's really no more room

Go and see the brothels
In that very famous town
Go and see the pinnacles
Where you just drive round and round

There's so much in Western Australia
Much more than I recall
So if you're going to go there
Please give me a call

Happiness

Happiness is something
You always give to me
Happiness is something
You always give for free

Happiness is something
You always make me feel
Happiness is something
You can give but never steal

Happiness is something
That comes straight from the heart
Happiness is something
We will never be apart

Happiness is something
I want the world to know
Happiness is something
I'm smiling, does it show

Happiness is something
I want us both to share
Happiness is something
That shows you really care

Happiness is something
That comes from deep inside
Happiness is something
When your arms are open wide

Happiness is something
When our lips together kiss
Happiness is something
With years of wedded bliss

Happiness is something
From you is really true
Happiness is something
In everything you do

On this, our anniversary
And it's only just the start
Of the times I say I love you
And they come straight from my heart

A Ten Dollar Tourist

We came here to Australia
In nineteen sixty eight
And soon after we arrived
I hoped we weren't too late

We came here to a land
Where we'd be safe and sound
Of vast great open spaces
Where we could own some ground

My wife and I and our four kids
Soon bought ourselves a house
Plenty of room and a big back yard
The kids thought that was grouse

As the years went by, the kids grew up
And they all got good careers
Then their Mum went back to England
That caused a lot of tears

But as they say, life goes on
And time heals all the pain
I met another woman
And I got married once again

We moved out to Tasmania
To start another life
We couldn't seem to make it work
And just had heaps of strife

We came back to the mainland
Were together twenty years
I should have separated long before
But it was loneliness I feared

I retired when I was sixty five
And I finally made the break
I left her with most we had
But I left for sanity's sake

Now I'm married for the third time
I'm happy and settled at last
The happiness I feel right now
Makes up for all that's past

I've been here more than fifty years
My life's not dull, but great
And I'd just like to tell you all
We never came too late

Travellers of the World

I only have one daughter
I mustn't say her name
And ever since that girl was born
Life was never quite the same

I love my daughter dearly
And I wish that I had more
But I'm satisfied with all my kids
My three sons make it four

When my daughter moved to London
She went to improve her life
Now she's married to a nice man
I'm sure she makes a lovely wife

They both of them run supermarkets
Work all the hours they can
Then her husband does the cooking
He must be quite a man

They've started travelling round the world
Venice was the last
They only go for a few days
Their life must be a blast

We talk a lot on the phone
We sometimes send a text
She tells me what their plans are
Where will they go next

Maybe they'll go to Iceland
Or somewhere just as cold
We wish they'd come to Australia
But I know what I'll be told

Family is so important
And I know we're far away
But I wouldn't change my way of life
For this is where I'll always stay

Lorraine and I send our regards
And hope you both are happy
But I can't forget that new born girl
Changing her shitty nappy

The Leprechaun

Have you ever seen a leprechaun
Little men dressed in green
They live down in the garden
Heard but seldom seen

They say they come from Ireland
A land across the sea
But now they're all around the world
Tormenting you and me

They're always playing little tricks
They live to just have fun
They live to make life joyful
They never hurt anyone

I'm told there's one quite near us
Through town, up the hill
Never short of a word or two
I'm sure he lives there still

He lives behind a property
If you care to go and see
I wouldn't say he's playful
But he hides from you and me

They live amongst the leaves
With a mushroom for a house
When they're running through the grass
They sound just like a mouse

They all look old
With a long grey beard
And you never see the children
That leprechauns have reared

They are special to the Irish
From legends, hundreds of years ago
I don't believe that they exist
But I don't want them to know

The Legend of a Famous Man

There is a man in town
That everybody knows
There's smiles and laughs and hand shakes
Where ever this man goes

His boyhood was in an orphanage
Near the town of Ballarat
Life was tough and really hard
But he made the most of that

Then he became a jockey
He won the Melbourne Cup
But just as he was getting the trophy
His wife came and woke him up

Soon he took up training
He really was quite good
He even taught Bart Cummings
As every trainer should

Now he is our own Father Christmas
With his suits of white and red
Of all the good things said about him
No more can be said

His yard is full of bottles and cans
There is no room to spare
He sells all these to make some money
His leisure time is rare

Whatever money this man makes
It's never for himself
It's other people's happiness
That gives this man his wealth

But there's one thing missing in his life
And as far as I recall
I've heard him say many times
I wished that I was tall

But I'd like to celebrate his lifetime
With all the good wishes that we send
I'm very glad to know this man
And I'm proud that he's my friend

Supermarket Hijinks

I went down to the supermarket
Found a place to park the car
It was pretty close to the entrance
So I didn't have to walk too far

I went to get a trolley
As any shopper would
But the rotten thing just wouldn't go
Where every trolley should

Whilst wandering up and down the aisles
I saw some funny sights
There stood a man with a long grey beard
Wearing women's tights

Then I saw a woman
With two children in her trolley
They kept on grabbing things
Did that woman do her lolly

Up came the manager
Said madam if you please
She said you mind your business
And hit him with the frozen peas

The manager called security
A mountain of a man
But her husband sat him in the ice cream
Picture it, if you can

Well the shop was in an uproar
Ice cream everywhere
The woman's kids running amok
I could only stand and stare

It was only then I realised
The man with the long grey beard
Was actually the woman's husband
No wonder that they're weird

The man then stood and stared at me
A fearsome looking man
Bugger all the shopping
I just turned and ran

A Family BBQ

I thought I'd have a barby
For some rellies and some friends
We've had some problems in the past
I'll try and make amends

They parked their cars out the front
As they started to arrive
We got the CD player all fired up
And the place became alive

I saw two people walking
They were only holding hands
They went behind the hay bales
I began to understand

I saw a man go in my shed
He was in there quite a while
Then I saw my Mum come out
I wonder why she smiles

I heard a ruckus in the barn
So I went and had a peep
I saw a couple in the straw
They certainly weren't asleep

What started as a barby
Turned out really good
With grown up people doing
What grown up people would

Then suddenly the sirens
And into our clothes we dived
But sadly it was too late
The police had just arrived

We're up before the Magistrate
He said we're silly goats
We should have found a better place
If we want to sow wild oats

Then just as we were leaving
He said we'd do no wrong
When next we have a barby
Invite the Magistrate along

Spirits of the Universe

Before the earth was even born
Eons of time ago
Spirits swam in the universe
Just how, we'll never know

They spoke to each other
By strength of thought
They planned to build the galaxies
With material they sought

After time immemorial
And all the planets born
Their skies were lit by lightning
Just the spirits showing scorn

When comets were formed
They would race through the sky
No creatures on earth
To see them go by

The earth was like mud
No land was as such
The spirits working by thought
And never by touch

Grain by grain the lands took shape
As the seas were formed by the rains
Earthquakes made the mountains
And the rivers formed the plains

The spirits kept working
Our galaxy done
They moved on to other worlds
Perhaps to have fun

To finish our world
It's just up to us
Learn to live peaceful
And not make a fuss

I hope we remember
What the spirits have done
Look after their work
Or else we'll have none

The Sorcerer

Can you imagine a sorcerer
Waving his magic wand
Turning people he doesn't like
Into frogs down in the pond

There are wicked kinds of witches
Who weave a magic spell
Torturing people they don't like
So they're not feeling very well

There are very handsome princes
Who give the frogs a kiss
Bringing back the princess
As all the people wish

But the sorcerer is always there
Worrying the village folk
Frightened of the cave he lives in
Their lives are not a joke

They seem to walk on eggshells
In the village they belong
They won't upset the sorcerer
They don't do anything wrong

But the sorcerer is wicked
He wants to make them hurt
It's nothing short of slavery
Living in the dirt

Then the villagers start to whisper
And begin to form a plan
To overthrow the sorcerer
And install a kinder man

They assembled at the cave mouth
And said for everyone's sake
We've installed a new magician
'Cos we've had more than we can take

Now the villagers are happy
There's nothing that they lack
But maybe someone's in the shadows
Making his plans to come back

Corellas Over the Bowling Green

I was working at the bowling club
Vacuuming the green
When a huge flock of corellas past
The biggest flock I've ever seen

They caused a great big shadow
As they passed by overhead
Then they left behind them
The parcels that I dread

I stood there looking around me
I couldn't believe my eyes
The green was covered in big white lumps
As they laughed with their raucous cries

They landed in the trees nearby
Making all this racket
While I got the bucket and brush
To clean up every packet

I worked very hard for the rest of the day
My back in so much pain
Then I saw their shadows
As they dumped it all again

I threw the brush over the fence
And the bucket in the air
I just didn't know what to do
I could only stand and stare

I had to fix this problem
But how I didn't know
The only thing I'm certain of
Those corellas had to go

I thought about it long and hard
To try and find a cure
I think I've solved the problem
Of all that bird manure

Now I'm working at the bowling club
I hear a loud report
It's just the folk from the gun club
Practising their sport

Easter

Well Easter time has been and gone
And the eggs have all been sold
All wrapped up in coloured paper
Red and blue and gold

They come in various sizes
From really big to small
But sadly there are children
Who don't get eggs at all

But it's not only eggs we buy
It's chocolate rabbits too
You can even buy a bilby
But they only make a few

They're made from different chocolates
From dark to milk, or white
The way some shops display them
It is an awesome sight

But there's one complaint I will make
They're on sale far too soon
And the way the shops are going
They'll be on sale in June

You know Easter's not just chocolate
There are other things too
Like the Royal Children's Hospital Appeal
I gave some, did you

Although the children love the chocolate
We have to be sincere
To the Royal Children's Hospital
And the lives that we hold dear

But Easter didn't start
When chocolate eggs began
There was another reason
A very religious man

When some Christians celebrate Christmas
They go to church and pray
That God, the lord and saviour
Will come back to us one day

Our Mailman

You have to admire our mailman
Delivering all our mail
He has to work in all the weather
In wind and rain and hail

He rides his motor scooter
He comes just once a day
But some of the mail he delivers
Are only bills to pay

It's not a very pleasant job
When the weather's really hot
But his motto is, the mail goes through
Whether its hot or not

He rides along the nature strip
Ducking under trees
He wished they'd cut the branches off
But they do as they please

I know the job's not easy
But he's done it many years
He's seen some sights as he goes round
Some laughter and some tears

He stops beside a letterbox
And a dog comes flying out
Barking, snarling and showing his teeth
Until you hear the owner shout

You see them round the shops in town
Pulling their trolley along
I'd never be able to do that job
I'm probably not that strong

He always smiles when I see him
He makes me feel much better
Especially when he delivers
That long awaited letter

This story's about our mailman
Just a rhyming tale
But I will have to go now
He's just delivered our mail

Out of this World

Would you like to be a space man
And fly up to the moon
Be just like an astronaut
And around the planets, zoom

Would you like to be real famous
And hear the people say
This man found alien life
Millions of miles away

You're captain of your rocket ship
Your crew are like your flock
The ship that you're in charge of
As big as an office block

To fly across the vastness
You're in cryonic state
When you reach your destination
You automatically awake

You climb aboard your landing craft
Go down and take a look
Discover worlds unknown to us
Like the famous Captain Cook

Most worlds you see are barren
With no water and no air
Just rocks and marks from craters
You soon get out of there

But some worlds are exciting
With still no sign of life
Volcanoes spewing sulphur fumes
You could cut them with a knife

Rarely do you find one
That's got insects and air
You do your tests and discover
You could really live up there

Eventually you're back on earth
You step from the ships air lock
The most famous person in the world
Or my name isn't Spock

All Mixed Up

I went to the dentist the other day
He said you've got pyorrhoea
I didn't like the sound of that
And developed diarrhoea

I went to the doctor and he said
The diarrhoea's still there
My diagnosis is correct
There's a pile of it by your chair

I said I couldn't help it
I'm ever so sorry doc
Then I bent down so I could
Tuck my trousers in my sock

He said you might have a very large problem
If you mix up your medication
You could get a stiffness in the mouth
That means oral constipation

But worse than that you could develop
On the lips of your bum, some teeth
That makes it really awkward
Trying to eat from beneath

I hurried home as best I could
Had a long talk with the wife
She said if you mix up that medication
You really are in strife

I thought how much my life would change
With a tongue I couldn't bend
And would the food taste any different
If I ate it from the other end

My normal life was over
Nothing worse it would seem
Then I woke with a start
It had all been a very bad dream

The Two of You

...A light hearted look at the bride and groom

Now TJ manages KFC
So there must be money in food
He's pretty young to be in charge
So he must be a really smart dude

It's said that TJ is keen on sports
And his Dad was just the same
We used to watch him race Triathlons
I thought that sport was pretty insane

Our TJ loves his garden
Grows the produce he can cook
But I wouldn't eat his cooking
I'd probably end up crook

But I'm told that TJ's very good
At everything he tries
Or is he just pulling the wool
Over everyone else's eyes

TJ loves to read and learn
And I think he's learnt a lot
So I'm a very lucky granddad
For the grandson that I've got

Now Ness is very clever
She's a nurse for the local vet
So guess where she takes TJ when he's ill
Not to the doctor, you bet

Ness is also a person who loves to read
From that she'd learnt many things
Like dogs can run because they've got legs
And birds can fly they've got wings...

It's said that Ness loves music
And really knows how to dance
She'd really like her TJ to learn
But TJ says not a chance

They both like to go out fishing
Take home and cook their catch
You can tell by just these few words
They must be the perfect match

I'm told they'd like to travel
Have the world at their beck and call
I imagine them on that balcony
As they stare at Niagra Falls

But think about ten years further on
There's a couple of kids running round
They still live on their place in town
It's the perfect place they've found

So we know that TJ and Ness are still married
And we know that their love runs deep
So when in the night our TJ says, Oh darling
Our darling says, go back to sleep

Now we wish you both a happy life
Full of laughter and no traces of strife
You'll raise your family healthy and strong
When ever that family comes along
And TJ be good to your wife

So I hope these words made you smile
And all our thoughts are with you
But from everyone here
We wish you good cheer
It's all hugs and kisses for you

So TJ shake your father's hand
And smother your mother with kisses
Then just feel very proud
That your Ness is now your missus

A Cheap Flight

I took a cheap flight overseas
It was a bumpy ride
I soon discovered why it was cheap
The toilets were outside

There are people sitting on the wings
Their faces covered in frost
I think if I ever go again
I won't consider the cost

Our pilot was a drunkard
And our flight was really risky
When the hostess served our coffee
He got a bottle of whisky

We were headed for Hawaii
The announcement said we're there
But we'd landed in Afghanistan
Which I didn't think was fair

They said, get back on board
We didn't walk, we ran
We should be soaking up sunshine
Not fighting the Taliban

Up in to the skies once more
I thought we would head back
But the pilot had got drunk again
And we landed in Iraq

American war planes fired on us
But they mostly shot each other
Our pilot gaily waved at them
But we just ducked for cover

We soon took off away from there
To somewhere much more grand
We wanted swaying palm trees
Not terrorists, rocks and sand

At last we reached our destination
But our joy did not last long
The agent forgot our visas
They sent us back where we come from

So if you're going on a holiday
And you want your money to go round
Why not think about Australia
Where you know you're safe and sound

The Soldier

As he put on his uniform
And stood there like a man
Tall, erect and courageous
As only a soldier can

He realised the time had come
When he had to go to war
To help to save old England
And even up the score

Soldiers coming home on leave
Said they couldn't believe the scene
Of the chaos that they saw there
And the German war machine

Our soldier was a paratrooper
Floating like a cloud
He landed amongst Canadians
And joined in with their crowd

They pushed on through the enemy
Up to the river Rhine
And there they met resistance
The last strong German line

With bullets and shells whistling
This army needs to win
Determined to cross the river
And then attack Berlin

Suddenly the shell exploded
Our soldier just felt sad
He'd never see his family again
That soldier was my Dad

Groesbeek Memorial is in Holland
Not far from where he died
He almost made it through the war
He died in March 1945

There's rows and rows of crosses
With not a single flower
Just his name on the memorial wall
ALFRED HERBERT GOWER